THE PSYCHOLOGY OF COMMUNICATION

George A. Miller

BASIC BOOKS, INC., PUBLISHER

New York · *London*

THE PSYCHOLOGY

OF

COMMUNICATION

Seven Essays

© 1967 by Basic Books, Inc.
Library of Congress Catalog Card Number: 67–17390
Manufactured in the United States of America
Designed by Jacqueline Schuman

Preface

The essays in this book treat a variety of topics—from cybernetics and automation to psychical research and the supernatural—but the diversity is largely on the surface. Underneath is a persistent concern with problems located at the intersection of scientific psychology and communication theory, concern with an attempt to formulate a psychological conception of man as an information-gathering, information-processing system. Perhaps such a conception of man seems too cognitive, too rational; it violates our twentieth-century recognition of the dark and irrational pyschological forces that break so easily through our outer wrappings of civilization. But an overemphasis on our blindly biological urges is just as wrongheaded as the eighteenth-century overemphasis on the powers of reason and social legislation. A balanced picture of man may begin on either side of this dichotomy, but it cannot ignore the other.

In an age when constraints on irrationality have worn thin, there are obvious reasons to begin with a reaffirmation of man's rational capacities. Of these capacities, man's versatility in communication is surely the most obvious and most important. The point was well stated many years ago by a great American social philosopher, George Herbert Mead: "The importance of what we term 'communication' lies in the fact that it provides a form of behavior in which the organism or the individual may become an object to himself." It is, Mead said, "when he not only hears himself but responds to himself, talks and replies to himself as truly as the other person replies to him, that we have behavior in which the individuals become objects to themselves." And the object which they become to themselves is, of course, their ego, their self, their identity. It is this addition of personal identity to the physiological organism that is so characteristic of human beings, that creates the frame of reference within which human psychologists must work, and it is a product of our human capacity for linguistic communication.

A psychologist who begins his study of man by examining the cognitive mechanisms of language and communication cannot be accused of beginning with some peripheral, unimportant, or oversimplified dimension of human nature. No other aspect so clearly separates man from all other species of animal, or is the source of so many peculiarly human strengths and weaknesses.

I hope the seven essays presented here will be viewed against this broad background of concern for our psychological conception of man. They span a dozen years and a variety of occasions. The first six are semi-popular pieces originally published elsewhere; the last and longest appears here for the first time. I thank the various publishers by whose permission these essays are reprinted in this volume. Only minor editorial changes and corrections have been made.

Most of these essays deal explicitly with psychological aspects of communication. Some reflect a communicative concern less directly. Memory, for example, is a communication from the past to the future, and the channel it travels from source to destination is often the human nervous system; the problem is to encode the message in such a way as to resist the ubiquitous noise that this channel introduces. Even the discussion of extrasensory perception is an essay on communication; on a putative form of communication over an unknown kind of channel. And the concern with computers—a computer is simply the most general possible case of an information-processing system, one that can transform the information in any describable manner before passing it on.

There is an inner consistency in the way these thoughts run through the various chapters. Or so it seems to me. I hope the unity that I feel to be here is something an attentive reader will recognize and be able to share.

George A. Miller

Cambridge, Mass.
June 1966

Contents

THE PSYCHOLOGY OF COMMUNICATION

1

Information and Memory

Some things are easy to remember. A short poem is easier to memorize than a long one; an interesting story is better recalled than a dull one. But brevity and wit are not all that is involved. Equally important is the way things fit together. If a new task meshes well with what we have previously learned, our earlier learning can be transferred with profit to the novel situation. If not, the task is much harder to master.

Imagine that you are teaching geometry to children. You have covered the business of calculating the length of the hypotenuse of a right-angled triangle when the base and the altitude are given. Now you are about to take up the problem of finding the *area* of a right triangle when the base and the hypotenuse are given. Suppose you were given your choice of the following two methods of teaching the children to solve the problem. In method A you would help them to discover that the area of a right triangle is half that of a rectangle with the same base and altitude, that the unknown altitude of the triangle in this case can be calculated from the given base and hypotenuse by use of the Pythagorean theorem, and that the area of the triangle can therefore be found by deriving the altitude, computing the area of the rectangle and then taking half of that. In method B you would simply tell the class to memorize six steps: (1) add the length of the base to the length of the hypotenuse; (2) subtract the length of the base from the length of the hypotenuse; (3) multiply the first result by the second; (4) extract the square root of this product; (5) multiply the positive root by the length of the base; (6) divide this product by 2.

Which method of teaching would you choose? Probably no one but an experimental psychologist would ever consider method B. Method A is productive and insightful; method B is stupid and ugly. But just why do we find method B repulsive? What is repugnant about a procedure that is logically impeccable and that leads always to the correct answer? This question is raised by the psychologist Max Wertheimer in his provocative little book *Productive Thinking*. An obvious answer is that a child taught by method A will understand better what he is doing. But until we can say what it means to understand what one is doing, or what profit there is in such understanding, we have not really answered Wertheimer's question.

It is helpful to consider the interesting fact that method B is the procedure we would use to instruct a computing machine of the present-day type. The machine is able to perform arithmetical operations such as addition, subtraction, multiplication, division and the extraction of roots. Instruction for the machine consists in writing a "program"—like the series of steps used in method B except that the computer's program must be even more explicit and detailed, with even less hint of the basic strategy. Computing-machine engineers have their hearts set on someday designing machines which will construct programs for themselves: that is, given the strategy for handling a problem, the machine will understand the problem well enough to create all the appropriate operations or subroutines required to solve it. The desirability of such a development is obvious. In the first place, at present it takes many hours of drudgery to write the detailed instructions for all the stops a computer must take. Then, after the instructions have been written, they must be stored in the machine in some easily accessible form. In a large machine the number of subroutines may run into the thousands; it might actually be more economical to equip the machine with the ability to create them on demand rather than to build the necessary storage and access machinery. In other words, in a very elaborate computer it would be more efficient to store rules from which subroutines could be generated than to store the routines themselves.

It seems, therefore, that even the computing machine realizes that method B is ugly. Each subroutine is an isolated operation that must be stored in its proper place, and no attempt is made to tie these steps to other information available to the machine. So we can see that one superiority of method A lies in the fact that it makes more efficient use of the capacity for storing information. In the teaching of geometry to a child, method A highlights the relations of the new problem to things that the child has already learned, and thus it provides the rules by which the child can write his own subroutines for computation. In essence the ugly method is less efficient because it requires the child to master more new information.

The intimate relation between memory and the ability to reason is demonstrated every time we fail to solve a problem because we fail to recall the necessary information. Since our capacity to remember limits our intelligence, we should try to organize material to make the most efficient use of the memory available to us. We cannot think simultaneously about everything we know. When we attempt to pursue a long argument, it is difficult to hold each step in mind as we proceed to the next, and we are apt to lose our way in the sheer mass of detail. Three hundred years ago René Descartes, in an unfinished treatise called *Rules for the Direction of the Mind,* wrote:

> If I have first found out by separate mental operations what the relation is between the magnitudes A and B, then that between B and C, between C and D, and finally between D and E, that does not entail my seeing what the relation is between A and E, nor can the truths previously learned give me a precise knowledge of it unless I recall them all. To remedy this I would run them over from time to time, keeping the imagination moving continuously in such a way that while it is intuitively perceiving each fact it simultaneously passes on to the next; and this I would do until I had learned to pass from the first to the last so quickly, that no stage in the process was left to the care of memory, but I seemed to have the whole in intuition before me at the same time. This method will relieve the memory, diminish the sluggishness of our thinking, and definitely enlarge our mental capacity.

Descartes's observation is familiar to anyone who has ever memorized a poem or a speech, or mastered a mathematical proof. Rehearsal or repetition has the very important effect of organizing many separate items into a single unit, thus reducing the load our memory must carry and leaving us free for further thinking. In terms of logic, the process is like the substitution of a single symbol for a longer expression which would be clumsy to write each time we wanted to use it.

The practical advantages of this unitizing process were vividly illustrated for me the first time I saw one of those digital computing machines that have small neon lights to show which relays are closed. There were twenty lights in a row, and I did not see how the men who ran the machine could grasp and remember a pattern involving so many elements. I quickly discovered that they did not try to deal with each light as an individual item of information. Instead, they translated the light pattern into a code. That is to say, they grouped the lights into successive triplets and gave each possible triplet pattern a number as its name, or symbol. The pattern all three lights off (000) was called 0; the pattern off-off-on (001) was called 1; off-on-off (010) was called 2, and so forth. Having memorized this simple translation, the engineers were able to look at a long string of lights such as 011000101001111 and break it down into triplets (011 000 101 001 111) which they immediately translated into 30517. It was much easier to remember these five digits than the string of fifteen lit and unlit lights.

Reorganization enabled the engineers to reduce the original complexity to something easily apprehended and remembered without changing or discarding any of the original data. There is an analogy between this simple trick and the process described by Descartes. Each step in a complex argument is like a single light in the binary sequence. Rehearsal organizes the steps into larger units similar to the engineers' triplets. Repeated rehearsal patterns the long argument into larger and larger units which are then replaced in thought by simpler symbols.

The first person to propose an experimental test of the span of a man's instantaneous grasp seems to have been Sir William Hamilton, a nineteenth-century Scottish metaphysician. He wrote: If you throw a handful of marbles on the floor, you will find it difficult to view at once more than six, or seven at most, without confusion." It is not clear whether Hamilton himself actually threw marbles on the floor, for he remarked that the experiment could be performed also by an act of imagination, but at least one reader took him literally. In 1871 the English economist and logician William Stanley Jevons reported that when he threw beans into a box he never made a mistake when there were three or four, was sometimes wrong if the number was five, was right about half the time if the beans numbered ten, and was usually wrong when the number reached fifteen. Hamilton's experiment has been repeated many times with better instrumentation and control, but refined techniques serve only to confirm his original intuition. We are able to perceive up to about six dots accurately without counting; beyond this errors become frequent.

But estimating the number of beans or dots is a perceptual task, not necessarily related to concepts or thinking. Each step in the development of an argument is a particular thing with its own structure, different from the other steps and quite different from one anonymous bean in Jevons' box. A better test of "apprehension" would be the ability to remember various symbols in a given sequence. Another Englishman, Joseph Jacobs, first performed this experiment with digits in 1887. He would read aloud a haphazard sequence of numbers and ask his listeners to write down the sequence from memory after he finished. The maximum number of digits a normal adult could repeat without error was about seven or eight.

From the first it was obvious that this span of immediate memory was intimately related to general intelligence. Jacobs reported that the span increased between the ages of eight and nineteen, and his test was later incorporated by Alfred Binet, and is still used, in the Binet intelligence test. It is valuable principally because an unusually short span is a reliable indicator of mental deficiency; a long span does not necessarily mean high intelligence.

A person who can grasp eight decimal digits can usually manage about seven letters of the alphabet or six monosyllabic words (taken at random, of course). Now the interesting point about this is that six words contain much more information, as defined by information theory, than do seven letters or eight digits. We are therefore in a position analogous to carrying a purse which will hold no more than seven coins—whether pennies or dollars. Obviously we will carry more wealth if we fill the purse with silver dollars rather than pennies. Similarly we can use our memory span most efficiently by stocking it with informationally rich symbols such as words, or perhaps images, rather than with poor coin such as digits.

The mathematical theory of communication developed by Norbert Wiener and Claude Shannon provides a precise measure of the amount of information carried. In the situation we are considering, the amount of information per item is simply the logarithm (to the base two) of the number of possible choices. Thus the information carried by a binary digit, where there are two alternatives, is $\log_2 2 = 1$ bit. In the case of decimal digits the amount of information per digit is $\log_2 10 = 3.32$ bits. Each letter of the alphabet carries $\log_2 26 = 4.70$ bits of information. When we come to make the calculation for words, we must take into account the size of the dictionary from which the words were drawn. There are perhaps 1,000 common monosyllables in English, so a rough estimate of the informational value of a monosyllabic word selected at random might be about ten bits.

A person who can repeat nine binary digits can usually repeat five words. The informational value of the nine binary digits is nine bits; of the five words, about fifty bits. Thus the Wiener-Shannon measure gives us a quantitative indication of how much we can improve the efficiency of memory by using informationally rich units. The computer engineers who group the relay lights by threes and translate the triplets into a code can remember almost three times as much information as they would otherwise.

It is impressive to watch a trained person look at forty consecutive binary digits, presented at the rate of one each second, and then immediately repeat the sequence without error. Such feats are called "mnemonic tricks"—a name that reveals the suspicious nature of psychologists. The idea that trickery is involved, that there is something bogus about it, has discouraged serious study of the psychological principles underlying such phenomena. Actually some of the best "memory crutches" we have are called laws of nature. As for the common criticism that artificial memory

The Psychology of Communication

crutches are quickly forgotten, it seems to be largely a question of whether we have used a stupid crutch or a smart one.

When I was a boy I had a teacher who told us that memory crutches were only one grade better than cheating, and that we would never understand anything properly if we resorted to such underhanded tricks. She didn't stop us, of course, but she did make us conceal our method of learning. Our teacher, if her conscience had permitted it, no doubt could have shown us far more efficient systems than we were able to devise for ourselves. Another teacher who told me that the ordinate was vertical because my mouth went that way when I said it and that the abscissa was horizontal for the same reason saved me endless confusion, as did one who taught me to remember the number of days in each month by counting alternately on and between my knuckles.

The course of our argument seems to lead to the conclusion that method A is superior to the ugly method B because it uses better mnemonic devices to represent exactly the same information. In method A the six apparently arbitrary steps of method B are organized around three aspects of the total problem so that each aspect can be represented by symbols which the student has already learned. The process is not essentially different from the engineers' method for recoding a sequence of binary lights.

It is conceivable that all complex, symbolic learning proceeds in this way. The material is first organized into parts which, once they cohere, can be replaced by other symbols—abbreviations, initial letters, schematic images, names, or what have you—and eventually the whole scope of the argument is translated into a few symbols which can all be grasped at one time. In order to test this hypothesis we must look beyond experiments on the span of immediate memory.

Our question is: Does the amount of information per item (that is, the number of possible alternative choices per item) affect the number of items we can remember when there is a large amount of material to be mastered? For example, is it more difficult to memorize a random sequence of one hundred monosyllabic words than one hundred digits or one hundred letters of the alphabet? The question is important because it has a bearing on how we can organize material most efficiently for learning.

In an exploratory study that S. L. Smith and I devised, the subjects were required to memorize three different kinds of lists of randomly chosen items. One list was constructed from a set of thirty-two alternatives (all the alphabet except Q plus the numerals 3, 4, 5, 6, 7, 8, and 9), another from a set of eight alternatives, and the third from just two alternatives. The subject read a test list at the rate of one item every second and then had to write down as much of the list as he could remember in the correct order. The lists ran to ten, twenty, thirty, or fifty items. If the subject failed to reproduce the list exactly, it was presented again. The number of presentations required before the first perfect reproduction measured the difficulty of the task.

We were not greatly surprised to find that the subjects did somewhat better (that is, needed about 20 per cent fewer trials) on the binary-choice lists than on the other types. After all, a run of, say, six zeros or six ones is easy to remember and therefore in effect shortens the list. But on the other two types of lists (eight alternatives and thirty-two alternatives) the subjects' performances were practically indistinguishable. In other words, it was just as easy to memorize a list containing a lot of information as one of the same length containing less information.

Very similar results have been obtained at the University of Wisconsin by W. J. Brogden and E. R. Schmidt, who did their experiments for other reasons and without knowledge of the hypothesis Smith and I were trying to test. They used verbal mazes with either sixteen or twenty-four choice points and they varied the number of alternatives per choice point from two to twelve. Here again the length of the list of points that had to be learned, and not the number of alternatives offered at each choice point, determined the difficulty of the test—with the same exception that we found, namely, that it was slightly easier to remember where only two choices were offered.

Tentatively, therefore, we are justified in assuming that our memories are limited by the number of units or symbols we must master, and not by the amount of information that these symbols represent. Thus it is helpful to organize material intelligently before we try to memorize it. The process of organization enables us to package the same total amount of information into far fewer symbols, and so eases the task of remembering.

How much unitizing and symbolizing must we do, and how can we decide what the units are? The science of linguistics may come to our aid here. Language has a hierarchical structure of units—sounds, words, phrases, sentences, narratives—and it is there that one should seek evidence for a similar hierarchy of cognitive units.

It has been estimated that English sentences are about 75 per cent redundant: that is, about four times as long as they would need to be if we used our alphabet with maximum efficiency. At first glance this fact seems paradoxical. If length is our major source of difficulty, why do we deliberately make our sentences longer than necessary? The paradox arises from a confusion about the definition of sentence length. Is a sentence one hundred letters, or twenty-five words, or six phrases, or one proposition long? The fact that all our books contain 75 per cent more letters than necessary does not mean that 75 per cent of the ideas could be deleted. And it is those larger subjective units, loosely called ideas, that we must count to determine the psychological length of any text.

A sequence of twenty-five words in a sentence is easier to recall than a sequence of twenty-five words taken haphazardly from the dictionary. The sentence is easier because the words group themselves easily into familiar units. In terms of psychological units, a twenty-five-word sentence is shorter than a sequence of twenty-five unrelated words. This means that the word is not the appropriate unit for measuring the psychological length of a sentence. Perhaps linguistic techniques for isolating larger units of verbal behavior will provide an objective basis for settling the question.

When we memorize a sentence, all our previous familiarity with the lexicon and grammar of the language comes to our aid. It is one of the clearest possible examples of the transfer of previous learning to a new task. And the transfer is profitable because it serves to reduce the effective length of the material to be remembered. By learning the language, we have already acquired automatic habits for unitizing those sequences that obey the rules of the language.

There are three stages in the unitizing process. All three were described in the seventeenth century by John Locke in his famous *Essay Concerning Human Understanding*: "Wherein the mind does these three things: first, it chooses a certain number [of specific ideas]; secondly, it gives them connexion, and makes them into one idea; thirdly, it ties them together by a name." Men form such complex ideas, Locke said, "for the convenience of communication," but the combination of ideas sometimes leads to confusion because it is "the workmanship of the mind, and not referred to the real existence of things." The development in the twentieth century of a mathematical theory of communication enables us to see more clearly how this process serves the convenience of communication and, coupled with the fact that it is the length not the variety of the material that limits our memories, gives us an important insight into the economics of cognitive organization.

Organizing and symbolizing are pervasive human activities. If we can learn to perform them more efficiently, perhaps we shall indeed be able, as Descartes promised, to "relieve the memory, diminish the sluggishness of our thinking, and definitely enlarge our mental capacity."

2

The Magical Number Seven,
Plus or Minus Two.
Some Limits on Our Capacity
for Processing Information

My problem is that I have been persecuted by an integer. For seven years this number has followed me around, has intruded in my most private data, and has assaulted me from the pages of our most public journals. This number assumes a variety of disguises, being sometimes a littler larger and sometimes a little smaller than usual, but never changing so much as to be unrecognizable. The persistence with which this number plagues me is far more than a random accident. There is a design behind it, some pattern governing its appearances. Either there really is something unusual about the number or I am suffering from delusions of persecution.

I shall begin my case history by telling you about some experiments that tested how accurately people can assign numbers to the magnitudes of various aspects of a stimulus. In the traditional language of psychology these would be called experiments in absolute judgment. Historical accident, however, has decreed that they should have another name. We now call them experiments on the capacity of people to transmit information. Since these experiments would not have been carried out if information theory had not appeared on the psychological scene, and since the results are analyzed in terms of the concepts of information theory, I shall have to preface my discussion with a few remarks about this theory.

INFORMATION MEASUREMENT

The "amount of information" is exactly the same concept that we have talked about for years under the name of "variance." The equations are different, but if we hold tight to the idea that anything that increases the variance also increases the amount of information we cannot go far astray.

The advantages of this new way of talking about variance are simple enough. Variance is always stated in terms of the unit of measurement—inches, pounds, volts, etc.—whereas the amount of information is a dimensionless quantity. Since the information in a discrete statistical distribution does not depend upon the unit of measurement, we can extend the concept to situations where we have no metric and we would not ordinarily think of using the variance. And it also enables us to compare results obtained in quite different experimental situations where it would be meaningless to compare variances based on different metrics. So there are some good reasons for adopting the newer concept.

The similarity of variance and amount of information might be explained this way: When we have a large variance, we are very ignorant about what is going to happen. If we are very ignorant, then when we make the observation it gives us a lot of infor-

The Psychology of Communication

mation. On the other hand, if the variance is very small, we know in advance how our observation must come out, so we get little information from making the observation.

If you will now imagine a communication system, you will realize that there is a great deal of variability about what goes into the system and also a great deal of variability about what comes out. The input and the output can therefore be described in terms of their variance (or their information). If it is a good communication system, however, there must be some systematic relation between what goes in and what comes out. That is to say, the output will depend upon the input, or will be correlated with the input. If we measure this correlation, then we can say how much of the output variance is attributable to the input and how much is due to random fluctuations or "noise" introduced by the system during transmission. So we see that the measure of transmitted information is simply a measure of the input-output correlation.

There are two simple rules to follow. Whenever I refer to "amount of information," you will understand "variance." And whenever I refer to "amount of transmitted information," you will understand "covariance" or "correlation."

The situation can be described graphically by two partially overlapping circles. Then the left circle can be taken to represent the variance of the input, the right circle the variance of the output, and the overlap the covariance of input and output. I shall speak of the left circle as the amount of input information, the right circle as the amount of output information, and the overlap as the amount of transmitted information.

In the experiments on absolute judgment, the observer is considered to be a communication channel. Then the left circle would represent the amount of information in the stimuli, the right circle the amount of information in his responses, and the overlap the stimulus-response correlation as measured by the amount of transmitted information. The experimental problem is to increase the amount of input information and to measure the amount of transmitted information. If the observer's absolute judgments are quite accurate, then nearly all of the input information will be transmitted and will be recoverable from his responses. If he makes errors, then the transmitted information may be considerably less than the input. We expect that, as we increase the amount of input information, the observer will begin to make more and more errors; we can test the limits of accuracy of his absolute judgments. If the human observer is a reasonable kind of communication system, then when we increase the amount of input information the transmitted information will increase at first and will eventually level off at some asymptotic value. This asymptotic value we take to be the *channel capacity* of the observer: it represents the greatest amount of information that he can give us about the stimulus on the basis of an absolute judgment. The channel capacity is the upper limit on the extent to which the observer can match his responses to the stimuli we give him.

Now just a brief word about the *bit* and we can begin to look at some data. One bit of information is the amount of information that we need to make a decision between two equally likely alternatives. If we must decide whether a man is less than six feet tall or more than six feet tall and if we know that the chances are fifty-fifty, then we need one bit of information. Notice that this unit of information does not refer in any way to the unit of length that we use—feet, inches, centimeters, etc. However you measure the man's height, we still need just one bit of information.

Two bits of information enable us to decide among four equally likely alternatives. Three bits of information enable us to decide among eight equally likely alternatives. Four bits of information decide among sixteen alternatives, five among thirty-two, and so on. That is to say, if there are thirty-two equally likely alternatives, we must make five successive binary decisions, worth one bit each, before we know which alternative is correct. So the general rule is simple: every time the number of alternatives is increased by a factor of two, one bit of information is added.

There are two ways we might increase the amount of input

information. We could increase the rate at which we give information to the observer, so that the amount of information per unit time would increase. Or we could ignore the time variable completely and increase the amount of input information by increasing the number of alternative stimuli. In the absolute judgment experiment we are interested in the second alternative. We give the observer as much time as he wants to make his response; we simply increase the number of alternative stimuli among which he must discriminate and look to see where confusions begin to occur. Confusions will appear near the point that we are calling his "channel capacity."

ABSOLUTE JUDGMENTS OF UNIDIMENSIONAL STIMULI

Now let us consider what happens when we make absolute judgments of tones. Pollack[17] asked listeners to identify tones by assigning numerals to them. The tones were different with respect to frequency, and covered the range from 100 to 8,000 cps in equal logarithmic steps. A tone was sounded and the listener responded by giving a numeral. After the listener had made his response he was told the correct identification of the tone.

When only two or three tones were used the listeners never confused them. With four different tones confusions were quite rare, but with five or more tones confusions were frequent. With fourteen different tones the listeners made many mistakes.

These data are plotted in Figure 1. Along the bottom is the amount of input information in bits per stimulus. As the number of alternative tones was increased from two to fourteen, the input information increased from 1 to 3.8 bits. On the ordinate is plotted the amount of transmitted information. The amount of transmitted information behaves in much the way we would expect a communication channel to behave; the transmitted information increases linearly up to about two bits and then bends off toward

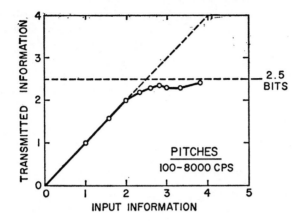

FIGURE 1. Data from Pollack[17, 18] on the amount of information that is transmitted by listeners who make absolute judgments of auditory pitch. As the amount of input information is increased by increasing from two to fourteen the number of different pitches to be judged, the amount of transmitted information approaches as its upper limit a channel capacity of about 2.5 bits per judgment.

an asymptote at about 2.5 bits. This value, 2.5 bits, therefore, is what we are calling the channel capacity of the listener for absolute judgments of pitch.

So now we have the number 2.5 bits. What does it mean? First, note that 2.5 bits corresponds to about six equally likely alternatives. The result means that we cannot pick more than six different pitches that the listener will never confuse. Or, stated slightly differently, no matter how many alternative tones we ask him to judge the best we can expect him to do is to assign them to about six different classes without error. Or, again, if we know that there were N alternative stimuli, then his judgment enables us to narrow down the particular stimulus to one out of $N/6$.

Most people are surprised that the number is as small as six. Of course, there is evidence that a musically sophisticated person

The Psychology of Communication

with absolute pitch can identify accurately any one of fifty or sixty different pitches. Fortunately, I do not have time to discuss these remarkable exceptions. I say it is fortunate because I do not know how to explain their superior performance. So I shall stick to the more pedestrian fact that most of us can identify about one out of only five or six pitches before we begin to get confused.

It is interesting to consider that psychologists have been using seven-point rating scales for a long time, on the intuitive basis that trying to rate into finer categories does not really add much to the usefulness of the ratings. Pollack's results indicate that, at least for pitches, this intuition is fairly sound.

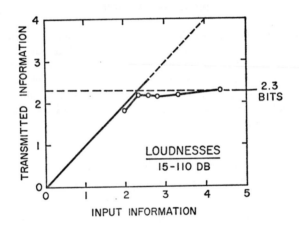

FIGURE 2. Data from Garner[7] on the channel capacity for absolute judgments of auditory loudness.

Next you can ask how reproducible this result is. Does it depend on the spacing of the tones or the various conditions of judgment? Pollack varied these conditions in a number of ways. The range of frequencies can be changed by a factor of about twenty without changing the amount of information transmitted more than a small percentage. Different groupings of the pitches decreased the transmission, but the loss was small. For example, if you can discriminate five high-pitched tones in one series and five low-pitched tones in another series, it is reasonable to expect that you could combine all ten into a single series and still tell them all apart without error. When you try it, however, it does not work. The channel capacity for pitch seems to be about six and that is the best you can do.

While we are on tones, let us look next at Garner's[7] work on loudness. Garner's data for loudness are summarized in Figure 2. Garner went to some trouble to get the best possible spacing of his tones over the intensity range from 15 to 110 db. He used four, five, six, seven, ten, and twenty different stimulus intensities. The results shown in Figure 2 take into account the differences among subjects and the sequential influence of the immediately preceding judgment. Again we find that there seems to be a limit. The

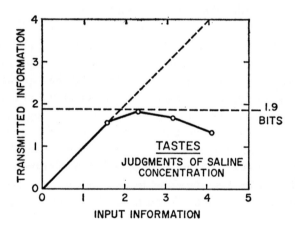

FIGURE 3. Data from Beebe-Center, Rogers, and O'Connell [1] on the channel capacity for absolute judgments of saltiness.

channel capacity for absolute judgments of loudness is 2.3 bits, or about five perfectly discriminable alternatives.

Since these two studies were done in different laboratories with slightly different techniques and methods of analysis, we are not in a good position to argue whether five loudnesses is significantly different from six pitches. Probably the difference is in the right direction, and absolute judgments of pitch are slightly more accurate than absolute judgments of loudness. The important point, however, is that the two answers are of the same order of magnitude.

The experiment has also been done for taste intensities. In Figure 3 are the results obtained by Beebe-Center, Rogers, and O'Connell[1] for absolute judgments of the concentration of salt solutions. The concentrations ranged from 0.3 to 34.7 gm. NaCl per 100 cc. tap water in equal subjective steps. They used three, five, nine, and seventeen different concentrations. The channel capacity is 1.9 bits, which is about four distinct concentrations. Thus taste intensities seem a little less distinctive than auditory stimuli, but again the order of magnitude is not far off.

On the other hand, the channel capacity for judgments of visual position seems to be significantly larger. Hake and Garner[8] asked observers to interpolate visually between two scale markers. Their results are shown in Figure 4. They did the experimenting two ways. In one version they let the observer use any number between zero and 100 to describe the position, although they presented stimuli at only five, ten, twenty, or fifty different positions. The results with this unlimited response technique are shown by the filled circles on the graph. In the other version the observers were limited in their responses to reporting just those stimulus values that were possible. That is to say, in the second version the number of different responses that the observer could make was exactly the same as the number of different stimuli that the experimenter might present. The results with this limited response technique are shown by the open circles on the graph. The two functions are so similar that it seems fair to conclude that the number of responses available to the observer had nothing to do with the channel capacity of 3.25 bits.

The Hake-Garner experiment has been repeated by Coonan

and Klemmer. Although they have not yet published their results, they have given me permission to say that they obtained channel capacities ranging from 3.2 bits for very short exposures of the

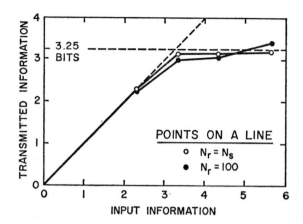

FIGURE 4. Data from Hake and Garner[8] on the channel capacity for absolute judgments of the position of a pointer in a linear interval.

pointer position to 3.9 bits for longer exposures. These values are slightly higher than Hake and Garner's, so we must conclude that there are between ten and fifteen distinct positions along a linear interval. This is the largest channel capacity that has been measured for any unidimensional variable.

At the present time these four experiments on absolute judgments of simple, unidimensional stimuli are all that have appeared in the psychological journals. However, a great deal of work on other stimulus variables has not yet appeared in the journals. For example, Eriksen and Hake[6] have found that the channel capacity for judging the sizes of squares is 2.2 bits, or about five categories, under a wide range of experimental conditions. In a separate experiment Eriksen[5] found 2.8 bits for size, 3.1 bits for hue, and 2.3 bits for brightness. Geldard has measured the chan-

The Psychology of Communication

nel capacity for the skin by placing vibrators on the chest region. A good observer can identify about four intensities, about five durations, and about seven locations.

One of the most active groups in this area has been the Air Force Operational Applications Laboratory. Pollack has been kind enough to furnish me with the results of their measurements for several aspects of visual displays. They made measurements for area and for the curvature, length, and direction of lines. In one set of experiments they used a very short exposure of the stimulus—$\frac{1}{40}$ second—and then they repeated the measurements with a five-second exposure. For area they got 2.6 bits with the short exposure and 2.7 bits with the long exposure. For the length of a line they got about 2.6 bits with the short exposure and about 1.0 bits with the long exposure. Direction, or angle of inclination, gave 2.8 bits for the short exposure and 3.3 bits for the long exposure. Curvature was apparently harder to judge. When the length of the arc was constant, the result at the short exposure duration was 2.2 bits, but when the length of the chord was constant, the result was only 1.6 bits. This last value is the lowest that anyone has measured to date. I should add, however, that these values are apt to be slightly too low because the data from all subjects were pooled before the transmitted information was computed.

Now let us see where we are. First, the channel capacity does seem to be a valid notion for describing human observers. Second, the channel capacities measured for these unidimensional variables range from 1.6 bits for curvature to 3.9 bits for positions in an interval. Although there is no question that the differences among the variables are real and meaningful, the more impressive fact to me is their considerable similarity. If I take the best estimates I can get of the channel capacities for all the stimulus variables I have mentioned, the mean is 2.6 bits and the standard deviation is only 0.6 bit. In terms of distinguishable alternatives, this mean corresponds to about 6.5 categories, one standard deviation includes from four to ten categories, and the total range is from three to fifteen categories. Considering the wide variety of different variables that have been studied, I find this to be a remarkably narrow range.

There seems to be some limitation built into us either by learning or by the design of our nervous systems, a limit that keeps our channel capacities in this general range. On the basis of the present evidence it seems safe to say that we possess a finite and rather small capacity for making such unidimensional judgments and that this capacity does not vary a great deal from one simple sensory attribute to another.

ABSOLUTE JUDGMENTS OF MULTIDIMENSIONAL STIMULI

You may have noticed that I have been careful to say that this magical number seven applies to one-dimensional judgments. Everyday experience teaches us that we can identify accurately any one of several hundred faces, any one of several thousand words, any one of several thousand objects, etc. The story certainly would not be complete if we stopped at this point. We must have some understanding of why the one-dimensional variables we judge in the laboratory give results so far out of line with what we do constantly in our behavior outside the laboratory. A possible explanation lies in the number of independently variable attributes of the stimuli that are being judged. Objects, faces, words, and the like differ from one another in many ways, whereas the simple stimuli we have considered thus far differ from one another in only one respect.

Fortunately, there are some data on what happens when we make absolute judgments of stimuli that differ from one another in several ways. Let us look first at the results Klemmer and Frick [13] have reported for the absolute judgment of the position of a dot in a square. In Figure 5 we see their results. Now the channel capacity seems to have increased to 4.6 bits, which means that

The Psychology of Communication

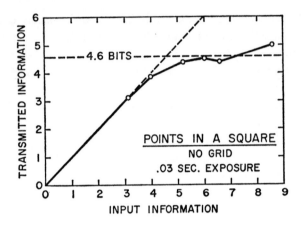

FIGURE 5. Data from Klemmer and Frick[13] on the channel capacity for absolute judgments of the position of a dot in a square.

people can identify accurately any one of twenty-four positions in the square.

The position of a dot in a square is clearly a two-dimensional proposition. Both its horizontal and its vertical position must be identified. Thus it seems natural to compare the 4.6-bit capacity for a square with the 3.25-bit capacity for the position of a point in an interval. The point in the square requires two judgments of the interval type. If we have a capacity of 3.25 bits for estimating intervals and we do this twice, we should get 6.5 bits as our capacity for locating points in a square. Adding the second independent dimension gives us an increase from 3.25 to 4.6, but it falls short of the perfect addition that would give 6.5 bits.

Another example is provided by Beebe-Center, Rogers, and O'Connell. When they asked people to identify both the saltiness and the sweetness of solutions containing various concentrations of salt and sucrose, they found that the channel capacity was 2.3 bits. Since the capacity for salt alone was 1.9, we might expect about 3.8 bits if the two aspects of the compound stimuli were judged independently. As with spatial locations, the second dimension adds a little to the capacity but not so much as it conceivably might.

A third example is provided by Pollack,[18] who asked listeners to judge both the loudness and the pitch of pure tones. Since pitch gives 2.5 bits and loudness gives 2.3 bits, we might hope to get as much as 4.8 bits for pitch and loudness together. Pollack obtained 3.1 bits, which again indicates that the second dimension augments the channel capacity but not so much as it might.

A fourth example can be drawn from the work of Halsey and Chapanis[9] on confusions among colors of equal luminance. Although they did not analyze their results in informational terms, they estimate that there are about eleven to fifteen identifiable colors, or, in our terms, about 3.6 bits. Since these colors varied in both hue and saturation, it is probably correct to regard this as a two-dimensional judgment. If we compare this with Eriksen's 3.1 bits for hue (which is a questionable comparison to draw), we again have something less than perfect addition when a second dimension is added.

It is still a long way, however, from these two-dimensional examples to the multidimensional stimuli provided by faces, words, etc. To fill this gap we have only one experiment, an auditory study done by Pollack and Ficks.[19] They managed to get six different acoustic variables that they could change: frequency, intensity, rate of interruption, on-time fraction, total duration, and spatial location. Each one of these six variables could assume any one of five different values, so altogether there were 5^6, or 15,625 different tones that they could present. The listeners made a separate rating for each one of these six dimensions. Under these conditions the transmitted information was 7.2 bits, which corresponds to about 150 different categories that could be absolutely identified without error. Now we are beginning to get up into the range that ordinary experience would lead us to expect.

Suppose that we plot these data, fragmentary as they are,

and make a guess about how the channel capacity changes with the dimensionality of the stimuli. The result is given in Figure 6. In a moment of considerable daring I sketched the dotted line to indicate roughly the trend that the data seemed to be taking.

Clearly, the addition of independently variable attributes to the stimulus increases the channel capacity, but at a decreasing rate. It is interesting to note that channel capacity is increased

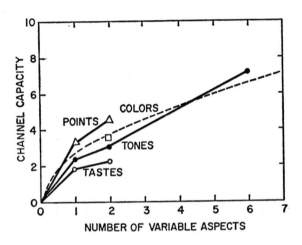

FIGURE 6. The general form of the relation between channel capacity and the number of independently variable attributes of the stimuli.

even when the variables are not independent. Eriksen and Hake [5] report that, when size, brightness, and hue all vary together in perfect correlation, the transmitted information is 4.1 bits as compared with an average of about 2.7 bits when these attributes are varied one at a time. By confounding three attributes, they increased the dimensionality of the input without increasing the amount of input information; the result was an increase in channel capacity of about the amount that the dotted function in Figure 6 would lead us to expect.

The point seems to be that, as we add more variables to the display, we increase the total capacity, but we decrease the accuracy for any particular variable. In other words, we can make relatively crude judgments of several things simultaneously.

We might argue that in the course of evolution those organisms were most successful that were responsive to the widest range of stimulus energies in their environment. In order to survive in a constantly fluctuating world, it was better to have a little information about a lot of things than to have a lot of information about a small segment of the environment. If a compromise was necessary, the one we seem to have made is clearly the more adaptive.

Pollack and Ficks's results are very strongly suggestive of an argument that linguists and phoneticians have been making for some time.[11] According to one linguistic analysis of the sounds of human speech, there are about eight or ten dimensions—the linguists call them *distinctive features*—that distinguish one phoneme from another. These distinctive features are usually binary, or at most ternary, in nature. For example, a binary distinction is made between vowels and consonants, a binary distinction is made between oral and nasal consonants, a ternary distinction is made among front, middle, and back phonemes, etc. This approach gives us quite a different picture of speech perception than we might otherwise obtain from our studies of the speech spectrum and of the ear's ability to discriminate relative differences among pure tones. I am personally much interested in this new approach.[15]

It was probably with this linguistic theory in mind that Pollack and Ficks conducted a test on a set of tonal stimuli that varied in eight dimensions, but required only a binary decision on each dimension. With these tones they measured the transmitted information at 6.9 bits, or about 120 recognizable kinds of sounds. It is an intriguing question, as yet unexplored, whether one can go on adding dimensions indefinitely in this way.

In human speech there is clearly a limit to the number of dimensions that we use. In this instance, however, it is not known whether the limit is imposed by the nature of the perceptual machinery that must recognize the sounds or by the nature of the speech machinery that must produce them. Somebody will have to do the experiment to find out. There is a limit, however, at about eight or nine distinctive features in every language that has been studied, and so when we talk we must resort to still another trick for increasing our channel capacity. Language uses sequences of phonemes, so we make several judgments successively when we listen to words and sentences. That is to say, we use both simultaneous and successive discriminations in order to expand the rather rigid limits imposed by the inaccuracy of our absolute judgments of simple magnitudes.

These multidimensional judgments are strongly reminiscent of the abstraction experiment of Külpe.[14] In that experiment Külpe showed that observers report more accurately on an attribute for which they are set than on attributes for which they are not set. For example, Chapman[4] used three different attributes and compared the results obtained when the observers were instructed before the tachistoscopic presentation with the results obtained when they were not told until after the presentation which one of the three attributes was to be reported. When the instruction was given in advance, the judgments were more accurate. When the instruction was given afterwards, the subjects presumably had to judge all three attributes in order to report on any one of them and the accuracy was correspondingly lower. This is in complete accord with the results we have just been considering, where the accuracy of judgment on each attribute decreased as more dimensions were added. The point is probably obvious, but I shall make it anyhow, that the abstraction experiments did *not* demonstrate that people can judge only one attribute at a time. They merely showed what seems quite reasonable, that people are less accurate if they must judge more than one attribute simultaneously.

SUBITIZING

I cannot leave this general area without mentioning, however briefly, the experiments conducted at Mount Holyoke College on the discrimination of number.[12] In experiments by Kaufman, Lord, Reese, and Volkmann random patterns of dots were flashed on a screen for one fifth of a second. Anywhere from one to more than two hundred dots could appear in the pattern. The subject's task was to report how many dots there were.

The first point to note is that on patterns containing up to five or six dots the subjects simply did not make errors. The performance on these small numbers of dots was so different from the performance with more dots that it was given a special name. Below seven the subjects were said to *subitize;* above seven they were said to *estimate.* This is, as you will recognize, what we once optimistically called "the span of attention."

This discontinuity at seven is, of course, suggestive. Is this the same basic process that limits our unidimensional judgments to about seven categories? The generalization is tempting, but not sound in my opinion. The data on number estimates have not been analyzed in informational terms; but on the basis of the published data I would guess that the subjects transmitted something more than four bits of information about the number of dots. Using the same arguments as before, we would conclude that there are about twenty or thirty distinguishable categories of numerousness. This is considerably more information than we would expect to get from an unidimensional display. It is, as a matter of fact, very much like a two-dimensional display. Although the dimensionality of the random dot patterns is not entirely clear, these results are in the same range as Klemmer and Frick's for their two-dimensional display of dots in a square. Perhaps the two dimensions of numerousness are area and density. When the subject can subitize, area and density may not be the significant variables, but when the subject must estimate perhaps they are significant. In any event, the comparison is not so simple as it might seem at first thought.

This is one of the ways in which the magical number seven has persecuted me. Here we have two closely related kinds of experiments, both of which point to the significance of the number seven as a limit on our capacities. And yet when we examine the matter more closely, there seems to be a reasonable suspicion that it is nothing more than a coincidence.

THE SPAN OF IMMEDIATE MEMORY

Let me summarize the situation in this way. There is a clear and definite limit to the accuracy with which we can identify absolutely the magnitude of a unidimensional stimulus variable. I would propose to call this limit the *span of absolute judgment*, and I maintain that for unidimensional judgments this span is usually somewhere in the neighborhood of seven. We are not completely at the mercy of this limited span, however, because we have a variety of techniques for getting around it and increasing the accuracy of our judgments. The three most important of these devices are (*a*) to make relative rather than absolute judgments; or, if that is not possible, (*b*) to increase the number of dimensions along which the stimuli can differ; or (*c*) to arrange the task in such a way that we make a sequence of several absolute judgments in a row.

The study of relative judgments is one of the oldest topics in experimental psychology, and I will not pause to review it now. The second device, increasing the dimensionality, we have just considered. It seems that by adding more dimensions and requiring crude, binary, yes-no judgments on each attribute we can extend the span of absolute judgment from seven to at least 150. Judging from our everyday behavior, the limit is probably in the thousands, if indeed there is a limit. In my opinion, we cannot go on compounding dimensions indefinitely. I suspect that there is also a *span of perceptual dimensionality* and that this span is somewhere in the neighborhood of ten, but I must add at once that there is no objective evidence to support this suspicion. This is a question sadly needing experimental exploration.

Concerning the third device, the use of successive judgments, I have quite a bit to say because this device introduces memory as the handmaiden of discrimination. And, since mnemonic processes are at least as complex as are perceptual processes, we can anticipate that their interactions will not be easily disentangled.

Suppose that we start by simply extending slightly the experimental procedure that we have been using. Up to this point we have presented a single stimulus and asked the observer to name it immediately thereafter. We can extend this procedure by requiring the observer to withhold his response until we have given him several stimuli in succession. At the end of the sequence of stimuli he then makes his response. We still have the same sort of input-output situation that is required for the measurement of transmitted information. But now we have passed from an experiment on absolute judgment to what is traditionally called an experiment on immediate memory.

Before we look at any data on this topic I feel I must give you a word of warning to help you avoid some obvious associations that can be confusing. Everybody knows that there is a finite span of immediate memory and that for a lot of different kinds of test materials this span is about seven items in length. I have just shown you that there is a span of absolute judgment that can distinguish about seven categories and that there is a span of attention that will encompass about six objects at a glance. What is more natural than to think that all three of these spans are different aspects of a single underlying process? And that is a fundamental mistake, as I shall be at some pains to demonstrate. This mistake is one of the malicious persecutions that the magical number seven has subjected me to.

My mistake went something like this. We have seen that the

invariant feature in the span of absolute judgment is the amount of information that the observer can transmit. There is a real operational similarity between the absolute judgment experiment and the immediate memory experiment. If immediate memory is like absolute judgment, then it should follow that the invariant feature in the span of immediate memory is also the amount of information that an observer can retain. If the amount of information in the span of immediate memory is a constant, then the span should be short when the individual items contain a lot of information and the span should be long when the items contain little information. For example, decimal digits are worth 3.3 bits apiece. We can recall about seven of them, for a total of twenty-three bits of information. Isolated English words are worth about ten bits apiece. If the total amount of information is to remain constant at twenty-three bits, then we should be able to remember only two or three words chosen at random. In this way I generated a theory about how the span of immediate memory should vary as a function of the amount of information per item in the test materials.

The measurements of memory span in the literature are suggestive on this question, but not definitive. And so it was necessary to do the experiment to see. Hayes[10] tried it out with five different kinds of test materials: binary digits, decimal digits, letters of the alphabet, letters plus decimal digits, and with a thousand monosyllabic words. The lists were read aloud at the rate of one item per second and the subjects had as much time as they needed to give their responses. A procedure described by Woodworth [20] was used to score the responses.

The results are shown by the filled circles in Figure 7. Here the dotted line indicates what the span should have been if the amount of information in the span were constant. The solid curves represent the data. Hayes repeated the experiment using test vocabularies of different sizes but all containing only English monosyllables (open circles in Figure 7). This more homogeneous test material did not change the picture significantly. With binary items the span is about nine and, although it drops to about five with monosyllabic English words, the difference is far less than the hypothesis of constant information would require.

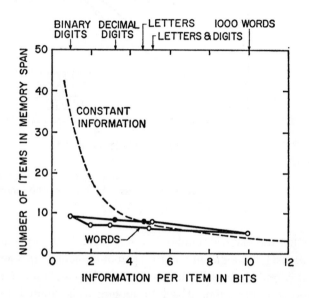

FIGURE 7. Data from Hayes[10] on the span of immediate memory plotted as a function of the amount of information per item in the test materials.

There is nothing wrong with Hayes's experiment, because Pollack[16] repeated it much more elaborately and got essentially the same result. Pollack took pains to measure the amount of information transmitted and did not rely on the traditional procedure for scoring the responses. His results are plotted in Figure 8. Here it is clear that the amount of information transmitted is not a constant, but increases almost linearly as the amount of information per item in the input is increased.

And so the outcome is perfectly clear. In spite of the coinci-

The Psychology of Communication

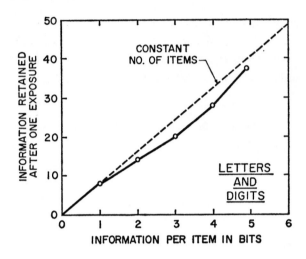

FIGURE 8. Data from Pollack[16] on the amount of information retained after one presentation plotted as a function of the amount
of information per item in the test materials.

dence that the magical number seven appears in both places, the
span of absolute judgment and the span of immediate memory are
quite different kinds of limitations that are imposed on our ability
to process information. Absolute judgment is limited by the
amount of information. Immediate memory is limited by the
number of items. In order to capture this distinction in somewhat
picturesque terms, I have fallen into the custom of distinguishing
between *bits* of information and *chunks* of information. Then I
can say that the number of bits of information is constant for absolute judgment and the number of chunks of information is constant for immediate memory. The span of immediate memory
seems to be almost independent of the number of bits per chunk,
at least over the range that has been examined to date.

The contrast of the terms *bit* and *chunk* also serves to highlight the fact that we are not very definite about what constitutes
a chunk of information. For example, the memory span of five

words that Hayes obtained when each word was drawn at random from a set of a thousand English monosyllables might just as appropriately have been called a memory span of fifteen phonemes, since each word had about three phonemes in it. Intuitively, it is clear that the subjects were recalling five words, not fifteen phonemes, but the logical distinction is not immediately apparent. We are dealing here with a process of organizing or grouping the input into familiar units or chunks, and a great deal of learning has gone into the formation of these familiar units.

RECODING

In order to speak more precisely, therefore, we must recognize the importance of grouping or organizing the input sequence into units or chunks. Since the memory span is a fixed number of chunks, we can increase the number of bits of information that it contains simply by building larger and larger chunks, each chunk containing more information than before.

A man just beginning to learn radio-telegraphic code hears each *dit* and *dah* as a separate chunk. Soon he is able to organize these sounds into letters and then he can deal with the letters as chunks. Then the letters organize themselves as words, which are still larger chunks, and he begins to hear whole phrases. I do not mean that each step is a discrete process, or that plateaus must appear in his learning curve, for surely the levels of organization are achieved at different rates and overlap each other during the learning process. I am simply pointing to the obvious fact that the dits and dahs are organized by learning into patterns and that as these larger chunks emerge the amount of message that the operator can remember increases correspondingly. In the terms I am proposing to use, the operator learns to increase the bits per chunk.

In the jargon of communication theory, this process would be called *recoding*. The input is given in a code that contains many chunks with few bits per chunk. The operator recodes the input into another code that contains fewer chunks with more bits per chunk. There are many ways to do this recoding, but probably the simplest is to group the input events, apply a new name to the group, and then remember the new name rather than the original input events.

Since I am convinced that this process is a very general and important one for psychology, I want to tell you about a demonstration experiment that should make perfectly explicit what I am talking about. This experiment was conducted by Sidney Smith and was reported by him before the Eastern Psychological Association in 1954.

Begin with the observed fact that people can repeat back eight decimal digits, but only nine binary digits. Since there is a large discrepancy in the amount of information recalled in these two cases, we suspect at once that a recoding procedure could be used to increase the span of immediate memory for binary digits. In Table 1 a method for grouping and renaming is illustrated. Along the top is a sequence of eighteen binary digits, far more than any subject was able to recall after a single presentation. In the next line these same binary digits are grouped by pairs. Four possible pairs can occur: 00 is renamed 0, 01 is renamed 1, 10 is renamed 2, and 11 is renamed 3. That is to say, we recode from a

TABLE 1. WAYS OF RECODING SEQUENCES OF
BINARY DIGITS

Binary Digits (Bits)	1 0 1 0 0 0 1 0 0 1 1 1 0 0 1 1 1 0								
2:1 Chunks	10	10	00	10	01	11	00	11	10
Recoding	2	2	0	2	1	3	0	3	2
3:1 Chunks	101		000		100	111		001	110
Recoding	5		0		4	7		1	6
4:1 Chunks	1010			0010		0111		0011	10
Recoding	10			2		7		3	
5:1 Chunks	10100				01001		11001		110
Recoding	20				9		25		

base-two arithmetic to a base-four arithmetic. In the recoded sequence there are now just nine digits to remember, and this is almost within the span of immediate memory. In the next line the same sequence of binary digits is regrouped into chunks of three. There are eight possible sequences of three, so we give each sequence a new name between 0 and 7. Now we have recoded from a sequence of eighteen binary digits into a sequence of six octal digits, and this is well within the span of immediate memory. In the last two lines the binary digits are grouped by fours and by fives and are given decimal-digit names from 0 to 15 and from 0 to 31.

It is reasonably obvious that this kind of recoding increases the bits per chunk, and packages the binary sequence into a form that can be retained within the span of immediate memory. So Smith assembled twenty subjects and measured their spans for binary and octal digits. The spans were nine for binaries and seven for octals. Then he gave each recoding scheme to five of the subjects. They studied the recoding until they said they understood it—for about five or ten minutes. Then he tested their span for binary digits again while they tried to use the recoding schemes they had studied.

The recoding schemes increased their span for binary digits in every case. But the increase was not so large as we had expected on the basis of their span for octal digits. Since the discrepancy increased as the recoding ratio increased, we reasoned that the few minutes the subjects had spent learning the recoding schemes had not been sufficient. Apparently the translation from one code to the other must be almost automatic or the subject will lose part of the next group while he is trying to remember the translation of the last group.

Since the 4:1 and 5:1 ratios require considerable study, Smith decided to imitate Ebbinghaus and do the experiment on himself. With Germanic patience he drilled himself on each recoding successively, and obtained the results shown in Figure 9. Here the

The Psychology of Communication

data follow along rather nicely with the results you would predict on the basis of his span for octal digits. He could remember twelve octal digits. With the 2:1 recoding, these twelve chunks were worth twenty-four binary digits. With the 3:1 recoding they were worth 36 binary digits. With the 4:1 and 5:1 recodings, they were worth about forty binary digits.

It is a little dramatic to watch a person get forty binary digits in a row and then repeat them back without error. However, if

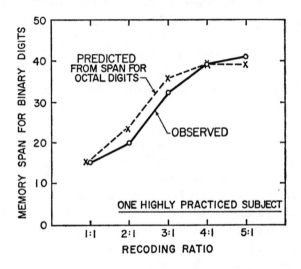

FIGURE 9. The span of immediate memory for binary digits is plotted as a function of the recoding procedure used. The predicted function is obtained by multiplying the span for octals by 2, 3, and 3.3 for recoding into base 4, base 8, and base 10, respectively.

you think of this merely as a mnemonic trick for extending the memory span, you will miss the more important point that is implicit in nearly all such mnemonic devices. The point is that recoding is an extremely powerful weapon for increasing the amount of information that we can deal with. In one form or another we use recoding constantly in our daily behavior.

In my opinion the most customary kind of recoding that we do all the time is to translate into a verbal code. When there is a story or an argument or an idea that we want to remember, we usually try to rephrase it "in our own words." When we witness some event we would want to remember, we make a verbal description of the event and then remember our verbalization. Upon recall we re-create by secondary elaboration the details that seem consistent with the particular verbal recoding we happen to have made. The well-known experiment by Carmichael, Hogan, and Walter[3] on the influence that names have on the recall of visual figures is one demonstration of the process.

The inaccuracy of the testimony of eyewitnesses is well known in legal psychology, but the distortions of testimony are not random—they follow naturally from the particular recoding that the witness used, and the particular recoding he used depends upon his whole life history. Our language is tremendously useful for repackaging material into a few chunks rich in information. I suspect that imagery is a form of recoding, too, but images seem much harder to get at operationally and to study experimentally than the more symbolic kinds of recoding.

It seems probable that even memorization can be studied in these terms. The process of memorizing may be simply the formation of chunks, or groups of items that go together, until there are few enough chunks so that we can recall all the items. The work by Bousfield and Cohen[2] on the occurrence of clustering in the recall of words is especially interesting in this respect.

SUMMARY

I have come to the end of the data that I wanted to present, so I would like now to make some summarizing remarks.

First, the span of absolute judgment and the span of immediate memory impose severe limitations on the amount of information that we are able to receive, process, and remember. By organizing the stimulus input simultaneously into several dimensions and successively into a sequence of chunks, we manage to break (or at least stretch) this informational bottleneck.

Second, the process of recoding is a very important one in human psychology and deserves much more explicit attention than it has received. In particular, the kind of linguistic recoding that people do seems to me to be the very lifeblood of the thought processes. Recoding procedures are a constant concern to clinicians, social psychologists, linguists, and anthropologists and yet, probably because recoding is less accessible to experimental manipulation than nonsense syllables or T mazes, the traditional experimental psychologist has contributed little or nothing to their analysis. Nevertheless, experimental techniques can be used, methods of recoding can be specified, behavioral indicants can be found. And I anticipate that we will find a very orderly set of relations describing what now seems an uncharted wilderness of individual differences.

Third, the concepts and measures provided by the theory of information provide a quantitative way to get at some of these questions. The theory provides us with a yardstick for calibrating our stimulus materials and for measuring the performance of our subjects. In the interests of communication I have suppressed the technical details of information measurement and have tried to express the ideas in more familiar terms; I hope this paraphrase will not lead you to think they are not useful in research. Informational concepts have already proved valuable in the study of discrimination and of language; they promise a great deal in the study of learning and memory; and it has even been proposed that they can be useful in the study of concept formation. A lot of questions that seemed fruitless twenty or thirty years ago may now be worth another look. In fact, I feel that my story here must stop just as it begins to get really interesting.

And finally, what about the magical number seven? What about the seven wonders of the world, the seven seas, the seven deadly sins, the seven daughters of Atlas in the Pleiades, the seven ages of man, the seven levels of hell, the seven primary colors, the seven notes of the musical scale, and the seven days of the week? What about the seven-point rating scale, the seven categories for absolute judgment, the seven objects in the span of attention, and the seven digits in the span of immediate memory? For the present I propose to withhold judgment. Perhaps there is something deep and profound behind all these sevens, something just calling out for us to discover it. But I suspect that it is only a pernicious, Pythagorean coincidence.

REFERENCES

1. J. G. Beebe-Center, M. S. Rogers, and D. N. O'Connell, "Transmission of Information about Sucrose and Saline Solutions through the Sense of Taste," *Journal of Psychology*, XXXIX (1955), 157–160.

2. W. A. Bousefield and B. H. Cohen, "The Occurrence of Clustering in the Recall of Randomly Arranged Words of Different Frequencies-of-Usage," *Journal of General Psychology*, LII (1955), 83–95.

3. L. Carmichael, H. P. Hogan, and A. A. Walter, "An Experimental Study of the Effect of Language on the Reproduction of Visually Perceived Form," *Journal of Experimental Psychology*, XV (1932), 73–86.

4. D. W. Chapman, "Relative Effects of Determinate and Indeterminate *Aufgaben*," *American Journal of Psychology*, XLIV (1932), 163–174.

5. C. W. Eriksen and H. W. Hake, "Multidimensional Stimulus Differences and Accuracy of Discrimination," *Journal of Experimental Psychology*, L (1955), 153–160.

6. C. W. Eriksen and H. W. Hake, "Absolute Judgments as a Function of the Stimulus Range and the Number of Stimulus and Response Categories," *Journal of Experimental Psychology*, XLIX (1955), 323–332.

7. W. R. Garner, "An Informational Analysis of Absolute Judgements of Loudness," *Journal of Experimental Psychology*, XLVI (1953), 373–380.

8. H. W. Hake and W. R. Garner, "The Effect of Presenting Various Numbers of Discrete Steps on Scale Reading Accuracy," *Journal of Experimental Psychology*, XLII (1951), 538–366.

9. R. M. Halsey and A. Chapanis, "Chromaticity-Confusion Con-

tours in a Complex Viewing Situation," *Journal of the Optical Society of America*, XLVI (1954), 442–454.

10. J. R. M. Hayes, "Memory Span for Several Vocabularies as a Function of Vocabulary Size," in *Quarterly Progress Report*, Cambridge, Mass.: Acoustics Laboratory, Massachusetts Institute of Technology, January–June, 1952.

11. R. Jakobson, C. G. M. Fant, and M. Halle, *Preliminaries to Speech Analysis* (Cambridge, Mass.: M.I.T. Press, 1952).

12. E. L. Kaufman, M. W. Lord, T. W. Reese, and J. Volkmann, "The Discrimination of Visual Number," *American Journal of Psychology*, LXII (1949), 498–525.

13. E. T. Klemmer and F. C. Frick, "Assimilation of Information from Dot and Matrix Patterns," *Journal of Experimental Psychology*, XLV (1953), 15–19.

14. O. Külpe, "Versuche über Abstraktion," *Bericht über dem I Kongress für experimentelle Psychologie* (1904), 56–68.

15. G. A. Miller and P. E. Nicely, "An Analysis of Perceptual Confusions among Some English Consonants," *Journal of the Acoustical Society of America*, XXVII (1955), 338–352.

16. I. Pollack, "The Assimilation of Sequentially Encoded Information," *American Journal of Psychology*, LXVI (1953), 421–435.

17. I. Pollack, "The Information of Elementary Auditory Displays," *Journal of the Acoustical Society of America*, XXIV (1952), 745–749.

18. I. Pollack, "The Information of Elementary Auditory Displays, II," *Journal of the Acoustical Society of America*, XXV (1953), 765–769.

19. I. Pollack and L. Ficks, "Information of Elementary Multidimensional Auditory Displays," *Journal of the Acoustical Society of America*, XXVI (1954), 155–158.

20. R. S. Woodworth *Experimental Psychology* (New York: Holt, 1938).

3

The Human Link in Communication Systems

I have the impression that some communication theorists regard the human link in communication systems in much the same way they regard random noise. Both are unfortunate disturbances in an otherwise well-behaved system and both should be reduced until they do as little harm as possible. Although these theorists, impressed by the inexorable laws of thermodynamics, have been forced to admit that noise is inevitable and inescapable, they still seem to believe that, if you are willing to take the trouble, the human element can be eliminated completely. This assumption, that man is not here to stay, is overly optimistic.

The fact that every communication system winds somewhere

The Psychology of Communication

home to a human nervous system means that no theory of communication will be complete unless it is capable of treating the system components in a theoretical language so general and so powerful that human beings can be included along with the other components. For many years the concepts of communication engineering were phrased entirely in the language of volts, amperes, ohms, watts, etc. These terms have limited value when we try to describe the behavior of a human being. They forced us to distort our picture of the human link in order to fit man into the rest of the system. So long as the concepts of communication theory had to be stated in these terms, the area of contact between electrical engineering and psychology was very limited indeed.

Today the relations between the science of communication and the science of psychology are vastly expanded, owing to the development of a way to measure information and a theory so general that we can truly say that any device, be it human or electrical or mechanical, must conform to the theory if it is to perform the function of communication. Today we are no longer required to think of the man as a voltage source, but can look at him as a source of information, or a channel through which information can flow.

I am proud to say that psychologists have not been slow to recognize the obvious fact that a large part of behavior is concerned with sending, transmitting, or receiving messages. In order to survive in a fluctuating environment, an organism must have some capacity to collect, process, and use information. This capacity is greatest in man, so that he is able to learn elaborate coding systems and to organize his social behavior by communicating with his fellow men. Thus communication is an important area for psychology; the development of a powerful, new theory of communication was bound to have important consequences for the study of human behavior. The ink was scarcely dry on Claude Shannon's "Mathematical Theory of Communication" before psychologists were applying the concepts in their psychological experiments. In the years that followed considerable data were amassed and a few tentative generalizations are now possible about man's capacity to handle information.

For example, we now know that it is impossible to predict how accurately a man will perceive a stimulus (for example, a word or a sentence spoken to him) on the basis of a physical analysis of the properties of that stimulus alone. It is necessary to know also what the other stimuli might have been from which this particular stimulus must be discriminated. A stimulus selected from a small set of alternatives may be correctly perceived even though exactly that same stimulus would not be perceived correctly if it were one of a large set of alternatives. This fact was not obvious to psychologists before we began to think in terms of information theory.

Suppose we consider the human being as a communication channel, with an input provided by the stimuli we present and an output consisting of his responses to these stimuli. To the extent that his responses depend upon and are correlated with the stimuli, the man acts as a communication channel. In order to measure his performance in terms of bits of information, we need to know three things: (1) the input probabilities, which are under the control of the experimenter and can be used to compute the amount of information in the stimuli; (2) the output probabilities, which can be estimated from the relative frequency with which the man makes each of the various alternative responses available to him and from which we can compute the amount of information in his responses; and (3) the joint probabilities for each stimulus-response pair, which can be estimated from the relative frequency of the occurrence of each response in the presence of each stimulus and from which we can compute the total amount of information we have when we know both the stimulus and the response. From these three measures of information we can quickly compute the amount of information that is common to both the stimuli and the responses. This common information

The Psychology of Communication

must have passed through the man's nervous system and so we take it to be the amount of information he has transmitted.

The psychological experiment is designed to give us estimates of these three classes of probabilities. First, a well-defined, finite set of alternative stimuli is selected by the experimenter. These may be digits, letters, words, tones, pictures, colors, or the like, depending upon the nature of the experiment. To each of these alternative stimuli a definite probability of occurrence is assigned; usually, all the stimuli are presented with equal probabilities. Second, a well-defined, finite set of alternative responses is selected. These may be motor responses to the keys of a piano or a typewriter; they may be vocal responses of naming or reading; they may involve writing, pointing, or moving some token, etc., again depending upon the purpose of the experiment. Third, the stimuli are then presented in a randomized order at a steady rate in time and the subject's response to each stimulus is recorded automatically. Finally, from a long sample of recorded data it is possible to estimate the necessary probabilities and to compute the amounts of information involved.

Numerous experiments following this general pattern have now been conducted. The most glaring result has been to highlight man's inadequacy as a communication channel. As the amount of input information is increased, for example, by increasing the size of the set of alternative stimuli, the amount of information that the man transmits increases at first but then runs into a ceiling, an upper limit that corresponds roughly to his channel capacity. This ceiling is always very low. Indeed, it is an act of charity to call man a channel at all. Compared to telephone or television channels, man is better characterized as a bottleneck. Under optimal conditions it is possible for a skilled typist or piano player to transmit about twenty-five bits per second. Until someone is clever enough to discover a way to do better, we shall have to regard twenty-five bits per second as near the upper limit. Even if we remove all time restrictions and permit a person to take as long as he needs to make a decision, he is unable to identify the stimulus without error when the stimulus is selected from a set of more than about a thousand alternatives. Thus we say that man's "span of absolute judgment" is probably on the order of ten bits of information per judgment. Needless to say, most of us operate most of the time far below these upper limits.

Perhaps man's particular skills in handling information have less to do with his speed of recognition than with his ability to remember what he has learned. This possibility raises many interesting questions which psychologists are presently unable to answer. For example, I know of no way to estimate the amount of information you have stored away in your permanent memory. However, it is possible to learn something about your "quick access" memory, the amount of information you can hold in mind at one time. And from the studies that have been conducted to date, I can report that you have no reason to be proud of yourselves. The amount of information you can think about at one time is hard to estimate, since it depends upon the particular way that the information happens to be encoded, but one hundred bits would be a representative figure. No self-respecting photographic plate would even bother to sneer at us.

It is my own opinion that man's peculiar gift as a component in a communication system is his ability to discover new ways to transform, or to recode, the information which he receives. It seems to me that the very fact of our limited capacity for processing information has made it necessary for us to discover clever ways to abstract the essential features of our universe and to express these features in simple laws that we are capable of comprehending in a single act of thought. We are constantly taking information given in one form and translating it into alternative forms, searching for ways to map a strange, new phenomenon into simpler and more familiar ones. The search is something we call "thinking"; if we are successful, we call it "understanding." It is possible that the development of high-speed digital computers

The Psychology of Communication

will soon strip even this last shred of dignity from the human mind.

In any case, it is quite clear that man is a miserable component in a communication system. He has a narrow bandwidth, a high noise level, is expensive to maintain, and sleeps eight hours out of every twenty-four. Even though we can't eliminate him completely, it is certainly a wise practice to replace him whenever we can. The kind of routine jobs that men like least are just the kind that machines do best. Our society has already made the first steps toward eliminating human bottlenecks from communication systems, and the years ahead are sure to bring many more.

This documentation of our worst suspicions about the human link in communication has, I believe, wider implications than are apparent from their obvious relevance to the traditional problems of psychology. For example, consider the fact that a human source cannot generate more than twenty-five bits per second for transmission over a voice communication system. As these systems are usually built, they have a channel capacity of somewhere between 10^4 and 10^5 bits per second. They are, in short, overdesigned by a factor of about four hundred to one. Since bandwidth and signal-to-noise ratio cost money, it is reasonable to ask why such a terrible mismatch of the channel to the source has been tolerated for so many years. Surely there must be some way to take advantage of the fact that a channel is going to transmit only human speech, and that it need not be designed for fog horns, bird calls, or symphony orchestras.

The problem to which I refer is generally known as the "speech-compression problem." It is an old problem, one that has engaged the attention of telephone engineers for at least twenty years. Homer Dudley's Vocoder was one of the earliest and still one of the most successful efforts to solve the problem. The Vocoder divides the speech spectrum into a number of adjacent frequency bands and transmits a signal representing the fluctuating level in each band. These band-amplitudes, along with a voicing signal and a pitch signal, suffice for the resynthesis of intelligible speech at the receiving end. The advantage of the Vocoder is that the signals can be transmitted over a narrow band of frequencies so that several conversations can be carried over a channel where only one could pass before.

When people listen to Vocoder speech they often complain that it sounds unnatural, and this may have led to the widespread belief that bandwidth compression necessarily loses "naturalness." Several years ago, however, Professor Fano described a perfectly feasible scheme that would reduce the necessary channel capacity by a factor of fifteen with no loss of naturalness. His suggestion was to transmit information about the amplitudes of the first twenty-eight harmonics, along with a signal indicating the fundamental frequency.

These ingenious schemes for bandwidth compression still fall short of the ultimate possible compression. If we are willing to tolerate speech that is intelligible but unnatural, there is a further factor of about twenty-five to one that we might still exploit. There is, of course, a big difference between speech that sounds natural and speech that is just intelligible. The Bell Telephone Laboratories have recently begun some interesting studies using the human being as a null device to detect changes in naturalness. What fidelity criterion does a listener use when he judges speech to sound natural? However, there are situations, particularly in military communication, where intelligibility is sufficient and naturalness is a luxury that can be sacrificed in the cause of greater efficiency. In such applications it is possible to simplify the speech wave and to transmit simpler signals that are equivalent in terms of the fidelity criterion necessary for intelligibility.

All bandwidth-compression schemes take advantage, in one way or another, of the properties of the signals that will be sent over the channel and of the nature of the fidelity criterion used by the receiver. Thus Fano, for example, wants to exploit the fact that the fundamental frequency of the voice ranges from about

125 to 250 cps, that the frequencies above the twenty-eighth harmonic carry little information, that the fluctuations in the amplitude of a particular harmonic are not more rapid than about 10 cps, and that the human fidelity criterion is relatively insensitive to the phase relations among the harmonics. By using just these simple facts about human talkers and listeners, he can transmit fifteen voices with the same channel capacity presently expended to transmit one voice. Now it is perfectly possible to go further and do better, but only on the basis of further and better information about the significant properties of speech and hearing. We need to know what modifications of speech leave intelligibility invariant. Now this is just the point. In order to take advantage of the special properties of speech and hearing, the communications engineer is going to have to join forces with the linguist and the psychologist to find out what liberties he can take in simplifying the signal without violating the listener's fidelity criterion for naturalness or his fidelity criterion for intelligibility.

There are several active groups in this country currently searching for the information-carrying core of the speech wave, and similar work is done in Japan, England, Sweden, and Russia.

Several years ago I became interested in the nature of the errors that people make when they listen to speech over noisy channels. For many years we have been conducting listening tests with speech as the stimulus. Words are spoken into a microphone, mixed with noise in controlled amounts, and then led to a listener's earphones. The listener writes the words that he thinks he heard, and his paper is later scored for accuracy. For most purposes, the percentage of the words that were heard correctly is a sufficient measure of the adequacy of the system. My curiosity was aroused, however, by the mistakes people made. If they didn't hear the word correctly, then what did they hear?

In order to study this question of errors, I selected a set of sixteen monosyllables that differed from one another only in the quality of their initial consonants: *pa, ta, ka, ba, da, ga, fa,* etc. The listeners memorized this list and were instructed to write down something, to guess if necessary, every time a syllable was spoken. Consequently, whenever they made a mistake, they gave me a record of their best guess as to what the sound might have been.

When we scored these tests we kept track of every possible stimulus-response pair. Since there were sixteen stimuli and sixteen responses, there were 16^2, or 256, stimulus-response pairs. These were recorded in the form of a 16-by-16 table which we called a "confusion matrix." Even a casual inspection of these confusion matrices showed that the errors did not occur at random. For example, *pa, ta,* and *ka* were often confused with one another, and *ba, da,* and *ga* were often confused with one another, but members of the first group were almost never confused with members of the second group. The configuration of errors that we observed was quite regular and appeared repeatedly on successive tests.

Now why, we asked, should this particular configuration of confusions occur? Sounds that are never confused must differ from one another in some important dimension that is very resistant to the masking effects of random noise. In order to discover what these features might be, we turned to the modern science of linguistics. There we found a classification of the English phonemes that accounted for practically all of the data we had collected. For example, linguists classify consonants as voiced or voiceless, depending upon whether the vocal folds are vibrating. We could summarize our data by saying that consonants which differed with respect to voicing were almost never confused. Or, to take another example, linguists classify consonants as nasal or oral, according to whether air is released through the nose or the mouth. Again, we found that nasality was very resistant to masking noises. But the feature which linguists refer to as "position of articulation," whether the consonant is produced in the front, the middle, or the back of the mouth, proved very susceptible to masking by even slight amounts of noise.

One immediate consequence of these results is that we know

better how to select special vocabularies for communication in high noise levels. We simply avoid any pairs of words that must be distinguished on the basis of place of articulation of some consonant, and we use only words that differ with respect to voicing or nasality. This practical application, however, is of less interest to us now than another, more theoretical outcome. Our data indicated that these different linguistic features of the English phonemes were perceived relatively independently. We are tempted to think of each feature as a separate signal sent from the talker to the listener. The problem, therefore, is to isolate the acoustic correlates of each linguistic feature, for then we can transmit very simple signals corresponding to these distinctive features of the phonemes.

There are about ten or twelve such distinctive features in English speech. Nearly all are binary in nature. At a rate of five phonemes per second, they would require a channel capacity of about sixty bits per second. In short, two hundred conversations over a channel that now carries one. It is a goal worth shooting for.

Several of the acoustic correlates of the distinctive features have already been isolated and equipment has been built that will extract the features from the sound wave. On the other half of the problem, machines are presently being developed that will take these signals and operate a typewriter or even synthesize intelligible speech for the listener. Some of the features are going to be hard to isolate acoustically, but it may be possible to place electrodes on the talker and pick up muscle potentials that are correlated with the production of those features that are acoustically obscure. Very little has been done with such nonacoustic signals, so it is hard to evaluate their usefulness.

Now the moral of my example is this. If you want communication equipment that will work, you can get it by being lavishly extravagant with channel capacity. But if you want to be efficient, to tailor your product to fit your customer, you will have to take a good look at your customer's dimensions. And if you join forces with psychologists in this attempt to take the measurements of mankind, I am certain you will find, as we have found, that the mathematical theory of communication developed by Norbert Wiener and Claude Shannon will be one of your most valuable tools.

In the end, therefore, I come back once again to the comparison with which I began. A human link and a source of random noise are both incorrigible disturbances in a communication system. In the case of noise, some of our best scientists have devoted themselves to analyzing it, measuring it, and avoiding it. The first step in reducing disturbances caused by noise is to find out the properties of the noise and then to take advantage of those properties by some clever method of encoding the message. My plea is simply that we should treat the man with equal respect. He cannot be abolished. But before we can take advantage of his peculiar fidelity criteria, we will have to find out more about him. Only then will we be able to provide channels of communication that are maximally efficient.

4

Concerning Psychical Research

If you dream that your dog is dying the same night a locomotive kills him, how do you account for it? If you see a person guess the order of a deck of cards far more accurately than chance would predict, what do you think he is doing? If you hear others describe similar improbable occurrences, what conclusions do you draw?

Such are the puzzles that motivate psychical research. In the eighty-odd years since the founding of the Society for Psychical Research, however, persistent inquiry by some extremely intelligent and imaginative people has failed to shed much light on the matter, and it has stirred up enormous argument and controversy.

The first question most of us ask ourselves is whether we should shrug these things off as interesting but fortuitous accidents or must assume that something unknown, perhaps something supernatural, causes them. Which is, at bottom, a very general kind of question. How improbable must an event be before we refuse to call it a coincidence? The answer to this more general question, as Thomas Bayes pointed out two hundred years ago, must depend on the a priori probabilities of any alternative hypotheses. Therein, I believe, lies a major source of the passionate debate that has surrounded this unorthodox branch of the scientific enterprise.

If we reject the hypothesis that nothing more than coincidence is involved, then a second question follows: What possible mechanisms might account for the reported phenomena? If not chance, then what? Most (but not all) of the incidents that have been reported could of course be explained if we were willing to assume that individual minds are not so well insulated from one another as most people believe. If we conclude that some such assumption is necessary, then what is the channel of communication, and why is it so terribly noisy? Is there some perfectly natural phenomenon at work that scientists have not yet discovered but that we may someday understand and control? Or have we here a phenomenon that is essentially incompatible with the fundamental laws and methods of physics? Or does this distinction make any sense at all?

The questions are not easy to phrase, much less to answer, and the darkness that surrounds them has not been relieved by the emotional reactions they seem to inspire. When as distinguished a philosopher of science as C. D. Broad agrees to wrestle with them (in his book *Lectures on Psychical Research,* published by the Humanities Press, 1962) we might hope at last to see the issues analyzed dispassionately and clearly set forth. Broad has lived a long time and has seen too many intellectual fashions come and go to be overly impressed by scientific prejudices. When he

The Psychology of Communication

turns his philosopher's gaze on the disreputable domain of psychical research, he is not easily intimidated by the collective disdain of hardheaded scientists. He knows all too well that most of these critics have not even examined the evidence, because, like the Aristotelians who refused to look through Galileo's telescope, they know in advance that there can be nothing to it. To such as these Broad can give as good a sneer as he gets.

Moreover, Broad brings knowledge to his task—detailed knowledge of the tangled history of many efforts to collect evidence relevant to the existence of psychical phenomena. This knowledge, based on years of active participation in the affairs of the Society for Psychical Research, led to his being invited to deliver the Perrott Lectures on the topic at the University of Cambridge in 1959 and 1960. The present book, which appears in the International Library of Philosophy and Scientific Method under the editorship of A. J. Ayer, amplifies the materials prepared for those lectures.

The list of Broad's qualifications must include more than courage and knowledge. As a student of the philosophical bases of modern science, Broad understands far more deeply than most psychical researchers the perils and pitfalls of inductive logic. These are displayed for the reader, along with the evidence and Broad's own pointed opinions, in lively, readable, interesting prose. The issues raised by psychical research are by no means clear or unambiguous; the analysis of these ambiguities is proper work for a person with Broad's philosophical interest and training.

The adjectives "courageous," "knowledgeable," "thoughtful" and "eloquent" describe both the man and his book. I almost wish "convincing" could be added to the list; it is uncomfortable to find oneself in disagreement with so gifted and persuasive an author. The most any skeptic must grant when he closes this book is not that paranormal phenomena exist but merely that we cannot prove that they do not exist. Which position falls considerably short of the one Broad himself has adopted.

Before reviewing the tiresome but still unanswered objections, I should outline the case Broad presents in support of his beliefs.

Psychical research is defined as the scientific investigation of ostensibly paranormal phenomena. Paranormal phenomena violate certain very general "basic limiting principles," mostly of a negative or restrictive kind, that are accepted without question by practically everyone raised under the influence of Western industrial society. Minds are private, the future must remain inscrutable, volition extends only to your own body, dead men tell no tales—these are examples of basic limiting principles. It is important to note that these principles are not necessarily laws of nature; to violate a basic limiting principle is not necessarily the same as to violate a natural law. Paranormal phenomena may result either from natural causes presently unknown to us or from supernatural causes whose nature may be forever unknowable; Broad's definition does not prejudge the issue. It is clear from the definition, however, that a belief in the reality of paranormal phenomena does not necessarily imply any belief in spiritualism; it entails no assumption that consciousness continues after death.

Psychical research, so defined, encourages an essential negative approach. When a reported incident seems paranormal, the psychical researcher must decide if any normal explanation can be given. Only if he fails to find a normal explanation can he classify the incident as paranormal—which places a heavy burden on his integrity and ingenuity in conducting the search for alternative explanations.

Ostensibly paranormal phenomena may occur sporadically (apparitions or phantasms, for example) or recurrently (haunted houses or communication through mediums). Sporadic instances do not lend themselves to experimental investigation, but they can be critically evaluated, classified and summarized. Recurrent phenomena will permit experimental controls and so may offer a better opportunity for answering some of the more puzzling questions that infest this whole domain of inquiry.

With his basic definitions out of the way, Broad turns next to the evidence. He first describes some of the classical experiments in guessing—those by S. G. Soal, by J. G. Pratt and Hubert Pearce, and by G. N. M. Tyrrell—in which certain people guessed the order of a haphazard sequence of events far better than chance would have led one to expect. In Soal's experiments, although sensitive guesses did not hit on the card the agent was thinking of at that instant, they did seem to hit on the card he would think of next (an example of precognition), but even that failed when any possibility of telepathy was eliminated. Pearce was able (at a distance of several hundred feet) to guess the order of cards Pratt merely handled but did not look at—which seems to exclude telepathy. Tyrrell constructed an elaborate electromechanical device that enabled him to randomize various conditions, but he got his best results when he did not know what alternative the machine would select (when telepathy was impossible) or when he did not press the keys in a strictly random order. The odds cited against the various observed outcomes occurring by chance are all impressively large, the largest being 8×10^{26} to one in the case of the Pratt-Pearce experiment.

Readers who do not enjoy statistical arguments will find this discussion tedious; those who do like statistics will find some looseness in Broad's treatment. His unqualified statement that the number of hits is normally distributed, his reference to a variance formula as a standard deviation, his neglect of the effects of optional stopping, his willingness to aggregate the improbabilities of selected sessions, his superficial explanation of correlation coefficients—all cast doubt on his level of statistical sophistication. And everyone will find it difficult to keep in mind which conditions seemed to work best for which agents and recipients, or to draw any general conclusion from the heterogeneous results. In spite of questionable statistics and conflicting results, however, I am personally willing to concede that something unlikely was observed in these guessing experiments.

The second section of the book deals with paranormal hallucinations and the logical puzzle of what one might possibly mean by a veridical hallucination. The evidence has a nineteenth-century flavor I associate with Grandmother's library. Take for example the Wilmot case. On February 21, 1890, W. B. H. of Bridgeport, Connecticut, sent to Richard Hodgson of the Society for Psychical Research a manuscript that W. B. H. had written from memory five years earlier. The manuscript recorded a story told by S. R. Wilmot concerning certain experiences had in 1863 by Wilmot, his wife, and W. J. Tait. The story, as later corrected by Wilmot and his wife, went as follows: Wilmot sailed from Liverpool in the ship *City of Limerick* in October, 1863. Ten days out he dreamed that Mrs. Wilmot, then at home in Connecticut, came to his stateroom clad in her nightdress. At the door she seemed to discover another occupant of the stateroom in addition to her husband, and she hesitated. Then she advanced to Wilmot's side, stooped down and kissed him, and withdrew from the cabin. The other person in the stateroom was Tait, who occupied the berth above Wilmot. When Wilmot awoke in the morning, Tait accused him of having had a lady visitor; questioning revealed that Tait, while lying wide awake in his berth, had witnessed a scene corresponding exactly to what Wilmot had dreamed. Moreover, when Wilmot finally arrived home, Mrs. Wilmot asked him whether he had received a visit from her on the night in question. She, it seems, had been lying awake in bed worrying about her husband's safety, until at about 4 A.M. she "went out to seek" him. It was as if she crossed a wide, stormy sea, came at length to a low, black steamer, somehow went up its side and descended into the cabin, and passed through it into the stern until she came to her husband's stateroom. She seemed to see a man in the upper berth looking right at her, and for a moment she was afraid to go in. Then she went up to the side of Wilmot's berth, bent down and kissed him, and went away.

"This," Broad comments, "is a very strange story. The only serious evidential weakness is that the first written report of it

The Psychology of Communication

depends on the memories of Mr. and Mrs. Wilmot as they were some twenty years after the date of the events reported." As regards Mrs. Wilmot, it is an *out-of-the-body* experience. As regards Tait, it is a waking *quasi-perception* of a *phantasm of the living*. As regards Wilmot, it was a paranormal *dream* whose contents corresponded with the simultaneous paranormal experiences of his wife and cabinmate. The case involves both *collective* and *reciprocal* visual *hallucinations*, which were *invasive* for Wilmot and Tait but *excursive* for Mrs. Wilmot. All in all, an excellent exercise in the lexicon of psychical research.

Why does Broad take such stories seriously? Obviously he believes in the integrity of his witnesses and the accuracy of their memories. More than that, however, he wants to believe them. As he admits, he has "a certain hankering after what I may call the 'mysterious' or the 'magical' and a strong desire that the current orthodoxy of many contemporary professional scientists (in particular experimental psychologists) may prove to be as inadequate as it certainly is arrogant and ill-informed." I believe, however, that the intellectual source of his confidence derives principally from the *Report of the Census of Hallucinations* conducted by the Society for Psychical Research and published in 1894.

The census was taken by 410 interviewers who asked about 17,000 persons this question: "Have you ever, when believing yourself to be completely awake, had a vivid impression of seeing or being touched by a living being or an inanimate object or of hearing a voice; which impression, so far as you could discover, was not due to any external physical cause?" Approximately 10 per cent of those interviewed answered this question in the affirmative. Of those who reported hallucinations, eighty gave reports of death coincidences, of which the psychical researchers judged thirty-two to be undoubtedly genuine. The total number of visual hallucinations of other people—including those that did not as well as those that did coincide with a person's death—was estimated to be about 2,100. In short, one in every sixty-three waking hallucinations about another person occurred within twelve hours of that person's death. On the basis of the death rate in England at the time, however, the fraction should have been only one in every 19,000 hallucinations if nothing more than chance were involved. "I think it is plain from these figures," Broad writes, "that there very probably is *some* connection, direct or indirect, normal or paranormal, between the occurrence of a waking hallucination of this particular kind and the occurrence, within a short period around that moment, of the death of the person referred to in the hallucination."

For those who relish a more-things-in-heaven-and-earth-Horatio philosophy, the third section of Broad's book is sure to be the most engrossing. Here Broad describes the performance of mediums: their trances, controllers, communicators, and remarkable utterances. Here we meet Mrs. Leonard, a professional but highly cooperative medium whose various voices were independently given word-association tests; Mrs. Willett, an amateur chosen specifically by the shades of F. W. H. Myers and Edmund Gurney as the channel through which they could describe their intricate psychical philosophy to Sir Oliver Lodge and Lord Balfour; Mrs. Warren Elliott, a professional who was carefully investigated by H. F. Saltmarsh, and Emmanuel Swedenborg, whose spiritual life was greatly enriched by some remarkable visions of the next world. As in the case of hallucinations, there are well-known psychological phenomena involved; in this case the relevant facts have to do with dissociated personalities alternately controlling the same human organism. Broad's main concern is not with abnormal psychology but with the question of veridicality: Does the medium accurately express ideas or information that could not have been known to her by normal means?

Consider the Vandy case. Edgar Vandy was an engineer and inventor, thirty-eight years old, who in August, 1933, died by accidental drowning. There was a certain amount of mystery as to the precise details of his death; Edgar's two surviving brothers,

The Psychology of Communication

George and Harold, were unsatisfied by the outcome of the inquest. George Vandy had no belief in survival after death, but he had been a member of the Society for Psychical Research and thought it possible that trance mediums might possess some kind of paranormal powers that would enable them to throw further light on his brother's last moments. Accordingly he sought the advice of Drayton Thomas, who recommended three mediums. The Vandy brothers went to all three, and in addition Drayton Thomas had a "proxy-sitting" for them with Mrs. Leonard. In all there were six sittings devoted to Edgar Vandy. Broad examines in some detail the content of those six sessions, particularly their accuracy and the remarkable degree of correspondence among them. Concerning Edgar's death, all six agreed that he fell and hit his head, and that one or more persons were present at the scene who might have saved him but failed to do so through cowardice or incompetence, but that Edgar wished to shield them. Five out of six sittings made reference to water and to drowning and stated that Edgar's death was a strangely unlucky event. Concerning the machine he had invented shortly before his death, four of the mediums gave information about it that, considering their general ignorance of such matters, was more or less accurate. "It is quite incredible," Broad says, "that the amount and kind of concordance actually found between the statements made by the various mediums at the various sittings should be *purely a matter of chance-coincidence*. . . . We must either suppose (without any direct evidence) elaborate fraud, in which the experimenter and the subjects must have collaborated; or we must admit the occurrence of modes of cognition which cannot at present be accommodated within the framework of accepted basic limiting principles."

The final chapter of the book—an epilogue on "Human Personality, and the Question of the Possibility of Its Survival of Bodily Death"—is a philosophical exercise in untangling terms and arguments. Broad bends over backward to present alternative possibilities and not final answers, but he points out that if one gives any credence to the mediumistic communications, they cannot *all* be plausibly accounted for by mere telepathy to the medium from persons still alive. His own view favors a dualistic solution of the body-mind problem: the psychic component of the medium's personality may be somewhat loosely combined with her body, which can thus become available to other psychic components. The psychic component of personality might be thought of as "a kind of highly complex and persistent vortex in the old-fashioned ether," which could persist for some time after bodily death but could have no new experience during the periods when it was not combined with the body of a medium. These ideas are presented merely as suggestions, not as conclusions. "For my part," Broad says, "I should be slightly more annoyed than surprised if I should find myself in some sense persisting immediately after the death of my present body. One can only wait and see, or alternately (which is no less likely) wait and not see."

How open must an open mind be? The history of science sparkles with geniuses who withstood and eventually overcame the entrenched prejudices of their day. Perhaps the advocates of paranormal phenomena also have hold of a higher truth; romantic sympathy for the underdog almost makes me hope they have. But in a world that has seen so much irrational nonsense accepted as truth, I can only set down my personal belief that this claim for the ultimate invasion of our privacy is fraudulent. An innocent fraud, perhaps, but no less vicious for its good intentions.

To which the reply may be, "But how do you explain . . . ?" I can explain nothing, of course. This failure might embarrass me more if psychical researchers offered any explanations I could not reject. But, as Broad points out, "to allege that a phenomenon is paranormal is to make a purely negative statement about it; it is not, in itself, to offer any kind of explanation of it." Indeed, there are no explanations to be had on either side of the argument; rational resolution cannot be expected from that direction at the present time.

The Psychology of Communication

In the absence of good arguments, therefore, let me raise two standard objections—the sampling problem and the problem of a priori probabilities—to justify my muleheaded satisfaction with the basic limiting principles of our society.

It seems to me that Broad underestimates the strength of the argument that in many instances there is nothing to be explained. When simplified, the demand for explanations seems to spring mainly from the improbability of the events that have been reported by psychical researchers. Improbability in and of itself, however, is no guarantee of paranormality.

If you continue to collect random data long enough, it is inevitable that something orderly will occur eventually; if you report only unusual occurrences, you can support any hypothesis that happens to appeal to you. Put it this way: Suppose you become seriously interested in psychical research. You undertake a prolonged and well-controlled experiment, let us say, in card-guessing. The results are inconclusive. Query: What will you do with your data? If you are like dozens of experimental psychologists I know, you will simply file them. You will probably not write them up and send them off to be published. I have no idea how many hundreds of failures had to go unreported before the handful of successes we know about could be obtained, but I am conscious of the considerable selectivity that underlies the reported results. Thus I am far less impressed than I should be, perhaps, when some gambler enjoys a remarkable string of good luck or some patient produces responses that correlate too well with an agent's random messages.

The dangers of selective sampling must not be underestimated. The time and effort that went into the *Census of Hallucinations*, for example, was largely wasted because of lack of adequate controls. The interviewers were people with an interest in the outcome; it is difficult to believe their respondents were not a specially selected subgroup. Broad himself, who is aware of all these objections but gives them far less weight than they deserve, remarks that a similar census should be conducted today with all the refinements that recent experience in taking Gallup polls would suggest, and hopes that "much more elaborate efforts would be made to ensure that those questioned constituted a fair sample." Until such a modern census is made, however, suspicion would seem the only rational attitude.

Many years ago a wise teacher told me that the really important question about telepathy is not is it true but why some people believe it is. At the time I thought he was prejudging the issue and I was surprised; he was not (in matters of science, at least) a bigoted man. Now I am not so sure. Perhaps what he meant was that it is impossible *not* to prejudge the issue.

Suppose that an experiment on telepathy is conducted without deliberate deceit or collusion, that appropriate controls are observed, that no mistakes occur in recording or analyzing the data, that impeccable use is made of probability theory—and still the correlation between the agent's and the patient's data is much closer than anyone would be willing to attribute to chance. Suppose, that is, we actually obtain bona fide evidence of communication between them. Now, even in this situation two choices are left open to us. We may be forced to grant that *something* went on between them, but we are not forced to grant that it was something paranormal. It is still possible that a perfectly normal chain of cause and effect was at work to produce the observed result.

How do we decide? Obviously we must eliminate every normal alternative hypothesis. This task is both painful and expensive, so that it may not always be pushed as far as it should be. In instances where the issue is important enough to justify the effort and expense, however, alternative explanations can often be found; I think of the debunking of "unidentified flying objects" as a case in point. But for each ostensible communication a new and specific explanation must be painstakingly established.

I suspect that many apparent instances of mind reading could be explained in terms of very subtle signals, perhaps unconsciously discriminated. It is tedious to keep insisting that tiny clues—tone of voice, hesitation, facial expression, eye movements, changes in breathing, muscular tensions—may suggest the performance the agent or experimenter wants; it would be even more tedious to collect evidence that such clues were effective in any particular instance. This is not an accusation of deliberate fraud; there is no question of dishonesty here. On the contrary, the problem arises because it is so terribly difficult to tell a lie, because there are so many different, but perfectly normal, channels of communication between people. No doubt psychical researchers have attempted to conceal their expectations, but this is an extremely difficult thing to do successfully. Broad admits such interactions are possible, but he thinks them less important than I do; that is, he assigns them a lower a priori probability.

The point is that one can usually imagine alternative hypotheses that do not involve paranormal phenomena, even though we may be in no position to state them explicitly. The fact that our experimental results were unlikely does not settle the question of what caused them to be unlikely. In this situation we are forced back on our a priori estimates of the probabilities of some rather vaguely phrased alternative hypotheses. For example, which is more improbable: that paranormal powers exist or that Mr. and Mrs. Wilmot did not remember precisely what happened twenty years before? Or again, which is more improbable: that Edgar Vandy's personality survived the death of his body or that the four mediums all had access to some other source of information? Even though we may admit that our card-guessing data could not have resulted by chance more than once, say, in a million times, we will still not believe in telepathy if we have already prejudged the existence of paranormal phenomena to be far less probable than that. There are some beliefs so strongly entrenched that no amount of statistical evidence can shake them.

The important question—as my teacher said—is not whether something remarkable occurred but whether you are prepared a priori to believe that what took place was paranormal. The kinds of evidence presented to date are not sufficient to settle the issue.

Of course, new evidence may be produced at any moment—nonstatistical evidence that will persuade even the most arrogant disbelievers. It is difficult to disagree with Broad when he writes: "It seems to me unlikely that there will be progress in the study of paranormal phenomena . . . unless and until someone hits upon methods of inducing paranormal powers in ordinary persons and sustaining them thereafter at a high level for some considerable time." Such an accomplishment would be a real breakthrough, in every sense of that overworked term.

I admit it may happen. But I wouldn't bet on it.

5

The Psycholinguists

Psychologists have long recognized that human minds feed on linguistic symbols. Linguists have always admitted that some kind of psycho-social motor must move the machinery of grammar and lexicon. Sooner or later they were certain to examine their intersection self-consciously. Perhaps it was also inevitable that the result would be called "psycholinguistics."

In fact, although the enterprise itself has slowly been gathering strength at least since the invention of the telephone, the name, in its unhyphenated form, is only about ten years old. Few seem pleased with the term, but the field has grown so rapidly and stirred so much interest in recent years that some way of referring to it is urgently needed. *Psycholinguistics* is as descriptive a term as any, and shorter than most.

Among psychologists it was principally the behaviorists who wished to take a closer look at language. Behaviorists generally try to replace anything subjective by its most tangible, physical manifestation, so they have had a long tradition of confusing thought with speech—or with "verbal behavior," as many prefer to call it. Among linguists it was principally those with an anthropological sideline who were most willing to collaborate, perhaps because as anthropologists they were sensitive to all those social and psychological processes that support our linguistic practices. By working together they managed to call attention to an important field of scientific research and to integrate it, or at least to acquaint its various parts with one another, under this new rubric.[1]

Interest in psycholinguistics, however, is not confined to psychologists and linguists. Many people have been stirred by splendid visions of its practical possibilities. One thinks of medical applications to the diagnosis and treatment of a heterogeneous variety of language disorders ranging from simple stammering to the overwhelming complexities of aphasia.[2] One thinks too of pedagogical applications, of potential improvements in our methods for teaching reading and writing, or for teaching second languages. If psycholinguistic principles were made sufficiently explicit, they could be imparted to those technological miracles of the twentieth century, the computing machines, which would bring into view a whole spectrum of cybernetic possibilities.[3] We could exploit our electrical channels for voice communications more efficiently. We might improve and automate our dictionaries, using them for mechanical translation from one language to another. Perhaps computers could print what we say, or even say what we print, thus making speech visible for the deaf and printing audible for the blind. We might, in short, learn to adapt computers to dozens of our human purposes if only they could interpret our languages. Little wonder that assorted physicians, educators, philosophers, logicians, and engineers have been intrigued by this new adventure.

Of course, the realization of practical benefits must await the success of the scientific effort; there is some danger that enthusiasm may color our estimate of what can be accomplished. Not a few skeptics remain unconvinced; some can even be found who argue that success is impossible in principle. "Science," they say, "can go only so far. . . ."

The integration of psycholinguistic studies has occurred so recently that there is still some confusion concerning its scope and purpose; efforts to clarify it necessarily have something of the character of personal opinion.[4] In my own version, the central task of this new science is to describe the psychological processes that go on when people use sentences. The real crux of the psycholinguistic problem does not appear until one tries to deal with sentences, for only then does the importance of productivity become completely obvious. It is true that productivity can also appear with individual words, but there it is not overwhelming. With sentences, productivity is literally unlimited.

Before considering this somewhat technical problem, however, it might be well to illustrate the variety of processes that psycholinguists hope to explain. This can best be done if we ask what a listener can do about a spoken utterance, and consider his alternatives in order from the superficial to the inscrutable.

The simplest thing one can do in the presence of a spoken utterance is to listen. Even if the language is incomprehensible, one can still *hear* an utterance as an auditory stimulus and respond to it in terms of some discriminative set: how loud, how fast, how long, from which direction, etc.

Given that an utterance is heard, the next level involves *matching* it as a phonemic pattern in terms of phonological skills acquired as a user of the language. The ability to match an input can be tested in psychological experiments by asking listeners to echo what they hear; a wide variety of experimental situations—experiments on the perception of speech and on the rote memorization of verbal materials—can be summarized as tests of a person's ability to repeat the speech he hears under various conditions of audibility or delay.

If a listener can hear and match an utterance, the next question to ask is whether he will *accept* it as a sentence in terms of his knowledge of grammar. At this level we encounter processes difficult to study experimentally, and one is forced to rely most heavily on linguistic analyses of the structure of sentences. Some experiments are possible, however, for we can measure how much a listener's ability to accept the utterance as a sentence facilitates his ability to hear and match it; grammatical sentences are much easier to hear, utter, or remember than are ungrammatical strings of words, and even nonsense (*pirot, karol, elat*, etc.) is easier to deal with if it looks grammatical (*pirots karolize elatically,* etc.).[5] Needless to say, the grammatical knowledge we wish to study does not concern those explicit rules drilled into us by teachers of traditional grammar, but rather the implicit generative knowledge that we all must acquire in order to use a language appropriately.

Beyond grammatical acceptance comes semantic interpretation: we can ask how listeners *interpret* an utterance as meaningful in terms of their semantic system. Interpretation is not merely a matter of assigning meanings to individual words; we must also consider how these component meanings combine in grammatical sentences. Compare the sentences: "Healthy young babies sleep soundly" and "Colorless green ideas sleep furiously." Although they are syntactically similar, the second is far harder to perceive and remember correctly—because it cannot be interpreted by the usual semantic rules for combining the senses of adjacent English words.[6] The interpretation of each word is affected by the company it keeps; a central problem is to systematize the interactions of words and phrases with their linguistic contexts. The lexicographer makes his major contribution at this point, but psychological studies of our ability to paraphrase an utterance also have their place.

At the next level it seems essential to make some distinction between interpreting an utterance and understanding it, for understanding frequently goes well beyond the linguistic context provided by the utterance itself. A husband greeted at the door by "I bought some electric light bulbs today" must do more than interpret its literal reference; he must understand that he should go to the kitchen and replace that burned-out lamp. Such contextual information lies well outside any grammar or lexicon. The listener can *understand* the function of an utterance in terms of contextual knowledge of the most diverse sort.

Finally, at a level now almost invisible through the clouds, a listener may *believe* that an utterance is valid in terms of its relevance to his own conduct. The child who says "I saw five lions in the garden" may be heard, matched, accepted, interpreted, and understood, but in few parts of the world will he be believed.

The boundaries between successive levels are not sharp and distinct. One shades off gradually into the next. Still the hierarchy is real enough and important to keep in mind. Simpler types of psycholinguistic processes can be studied rather intensively; already we know much about hearing and matching. Accepting and interpreting are just now coming into scientific focus. Understanding is still over the horizon, and pragmatic questions involving belief systems are presently so vague as to be hardly worth asking. But the whole range of processes must be included in any adequate definition of psycholinguistics.

I phrased the description of these various psycholinguistic processes in terms of a listener; the question inevitably arises as to whether a different hierarchy is required to describe the speaker. One problem a psycholinguist faces is to decide whether speaking and listening are two separate abilities, co-ordinate but distinct, or whether they are merely different manifestations of a single linguistic faculty.

The mouth and ear are different organs; at the simplest levels we must distinguish hearing and matching from vocalizing and speaking. At more complex levels it is less easy to decide whether the two abilities are distinct. At some point they must converge, if only to explain why it is so difficult to speak and listen simultaneously. The question is where.

It is easy to demonstrate how important to a speaker is the sound of his own voice. If his speech is delayed a fifth of a second, amplified, and fed back into his own ears, the voice-ear asynchrony can be devastating to the motor skills of articulate speech. It is more difficult, however, to demonstrate that the same linguistic competence required for speaking is also involved in processing the speech of others.

Recently Morris Halle and Kenneth Stevens of the Massachusetts Institute of Technology revived a suggestion made by Wilhelm von Humboldt over a century ago.[7] Suppose we accept the notion that a listener recognizes what he hears by comparing it with some internal representation. To the extent that a match can be obtained, the input is accepted and interpreted. One trouble with this hypothesis, however, is that a listener must be ready to recognize any one of an enormous number of different sentences. It is inconceivable that a separate internal representation for each of them could be stored in his memory in advance. Halle and Stevens suggest that these internal representations must be generated as they are needed by following the same generative rules that are normally used in producing speech. In this way the rules of the language are incorporated into the theory only once, in a generative form; they need not be learned once by the ear and again by the tongue. This is a theory of a language user, not of a speaker or a listener alone.

The listener begins with a guess about the input. On that basis he generates an internal matching signal. The first attempt will probably be in error; if so, the mismatch is reported and used as a basis for a next guess, which should be closer. This cycle

The Psychology of Communication

repeats (unconsciously, almost certainly) until a satisfactory (not necessarily a correct) match is obtained, at which point the next segment of speech is scanned and matched, etc. The output is not a transformed version of the input; it is the program that was followed to generate the matching representation.

The perceptual categories available to such a system are defined by the generative rules at its disposal. It is also reasonably obvious that its efficiency is critically dependent on the quality of the initial guess. If this guess is close, an iterative process can converge rapidly; if not, the listener will be unable to keep pace with the rapid flow of conversational speech.

A listener's first guess probably derives in part from syntactic markers in the form of intonation, inflection, suffixes, etc., and in part from his general knowledge of the semantic and situational context. Syntactic cues indicate how the input is to be grouped and which words function together; semantic and contextual contributions are more difficult to characterize, but must somehow enable him to limit the range of possible words that he can expect to hear.

How he is able to do this is an utter mystery, but the fact that he can do it is easily demonstrated.

The English psychologist David Bruce recorded a set of ordinary sentences and played them in the presence of noise so intense that the voice was just audible but not intelligible.[8] He told his listeners that these were sentences on some general topic— sports, say—and asked them to repeat what they heard. He then told them they would hear more sentences on a different topic, which they were also to repeat. This was done several times. Each time the listeners repeated sentences appropriate to the topic announced in advance. When at the end of the experiment Bruce told them they had heard the same recording every time—all he had changed was the topic they were given—most listeners were unable to believe it.

With an advance hypothesis about what the message will be

we can tune our perceptual system to favor certain interpretations and reject others. This fact is no proof of a generative process in speech perception, but it does emphasize the important role of context. For most theories of speech perception the facilitation provided by context is merely a fortunate though rather complicated fact. For a generative theory it is essential.

Note that generative theories do not assume that a listener must be able to articulate the sounds he recognizes, but merely that he be able to generate some internal representation to match the input. In this respect a generative theory differs from a motor theory (such as that of Sir Richard Paget) which assumes that we can identify only those utterances we are capable of producing ourselves. There is some rather compelling evidence against a motor theory. The American psychologist Eric Lenneberg has described the case of an eight-year-old boy with congenital anarthria; despite his complete inability to speak, the boy acquired an excellent ability to understand language.[9] Moreover, it is a common observation that utterances can be understood by young children before they are able to produce them. A motor theory of speech perception draws too close a parallel between our two capacities as users of language. Even so, the two are more closely integrated than most people realize.

I have already offered the opinion that productivity sets the central problem for the psycholinguist and have even referred to it indirectly by arguing that we can produce too many different sentences to store them all in memory. The issue can be postponed no longer.

To make the problem plain, consider an example on the level of individual words. For several days I carried in my pocket a small white card on which was typed UNDERSTANDER. On suitable occasions I would hand it to someone. "How do you pronounce this?" I asked.

He pronounced it.

"Is it an English word?"

The Psychology of Communication

He hesitated. "I haven't seen it used very much. I'm not sure."

"Do you know what it means?"

"I suppose it means 'one who understands.' "

I thanked him and changed the subject.

Of course, understander *is* an English word, but to find it you must look in a large dictionary where you will probably read that it is "now rare." Rare enough, I think, for none of my respondents to have seen it before. Nevertheless, they all answered in the same way. Nobody seemed surprised. Nobody wondered how he could understand and pronounce a word without knowing whether it was a word. Everybody put the main stress on the third syllable and constructed a meaning from the verb "to understand" and the agentive suffix -*er*. Familiar morphological rules of English were applied as a matter of course, even though the combination was completely novel.

Probably no one but a psycholinguist captured by the ingenuous behavioristic theory that words are vocal responses conditioned to occur in the presence of appropriate stimuli would find anything exceptional in this. Since none of my friends had seen the word before, and so could not have been "conditioned" to give the responses they did, how would this theory account for their "verbal behavior"? Advocates of a conditioning theory of meaning —and there are several distinguished scientists among them— would probably explain linguistic productivity in terms of "conditioned generalizations." * They could argue that my respondents had been conditioned to the word understand and to the suffix -*er;* responses to their union could conceivably be counted as instances of stimulus generalization. In this way, novel responses could occur without special training.

Although a surprising amount of psychological ingenuity has

---

* A dog conditioned to salivate at the sound of a tone will also salivate, though less copiously, at the sound of similar tones, the magnitude declining as the new tones become less similar to the original. This phenomenon is called "stimulus generalization."

been invested in this kind of argument, it is difficult to estimate its value. No one has carried the theory through for all the related combinations that must be explained simultaneously. One can speculate, however, that there would have to be many different kinds of generalization, each with a carefully defined range of applicability. For example, it would be necessary to explain why "understander" is acceptable, whereas "erunderstand" is not. Worked out in detail, such a theory would become a sort of Pavlovian paraphrase of a linguistic description. Of course, if one believes there is some essential difference between behavior governed by conditioned habits and behavior governed by rules, the paraphrase could never be more than a vast intellectual pun.

Original combinations of elements are the life blood of language. It is our ability to produce and comprehend such novelties that makes language so ubiquitously useful. As psychologists have become more seriously interested in the cognitive processes that language entails, they have been forced to recognize that the fundamental puzzle is not our ability to associate vocal noises with perceptual objects, but rather our combinatorial productivity— our ability to understand an unlimited diversity of utterances never heard before and to produce an equal variety of utterances similarly intelligible to other members of our speech community. Faced with this problem, concepts borrowed from conditioning theory seem not so much invalid as totally inadequate.

Some idea of the relative magnitudes of what we might call the productive as opposed to the reproductive components of any psycholinguistic theory is provided by statistical studies of language. A few numbers can reinforce the point. If you interrupt a speaker at some randomly chosen instant, there will be, on the average, about ten words that form grammatical and meaningful continuations. Often only one word is admissible and sometimes there are thousands, but on the average it works out to about ten. (If you think this estimate too low, I will not object; larger estimates strengthen the argument.) A simple English sentence can easily run to a length of twenty words, so elementary arithmetic tells us that there must be at least 10^{20} such sentences that a person who knows English must know how to deal with. Compare this productive potential with the 10^4 or 10^5 individual words we know—the reproductive component of our theory—and the discrepancy is dramatically illustrated. Putting it differently, it would take 100,000,000,000 centuries (one thousand times the estimated age of the earth) to utter all the admissible twenty-word sentences of English. Thus, the probability that you might have heard any particular twenty-word sentence before is negligible. Unless it is a cliché, every sentence must come to you as a novel combination of morphemes. Yet you can interpret it at once if you know the English language.

With these facts in mind it is impossible to argue that we learn to understand sentences from teachers who have pronounced each one and explained what it meant. What we have learned are not particular strings of words, but *rules* for generating admissible strings of words.

Consider what it means to follow a rule; this consideration shifts the discussion of psycholinguistics into very difficult territory. The nature of rules has been a central concern of modern philosophy and perhaps no analysis has been more influential than Ludwig Wittgenstein's. Wittgenstein remarked that the most characteristic thing we can say about "rule-governed behavior" is that the person who knows the rules knows whether he is proceeding correctly or incorrectly. Although he may not be able to formulate the rules explicitly, he knows what it is to make a mistake. If this remark is accepted, we must ask ourselves whether an animal that has been conditioned is privy to any such knowledge about the correctness of what he is doing. Perhaps such a degree of insight could be achieved by the great apes, but surely not by all the various species that can acquire conditioned reflexes. On this basis alone it would seem necessary to preserve a distinction between conditioning and learning rules.

As psychologists have learned to appreciate the complexities of language, the prospect of reducing it to the laws of behavior so carefully studied in lower animals has grown increasingly remote. We have been forced more and more into a position that non-psychologists probably take for granted, namely, that language is rule-governed behavior characterized by enormous flexibility and freedom of choice.

Obvious as this conclusion may seem, it has important implications for any scientific theory of language. If rules involve the concepts of right and wrong, they introduce a normative aspect that has always been avoided in the natural sciences. One hears repeatedly that the scientist's ability to suppress normative judgments about his subject matter enables him to see the world objectively, as it really is. To admit that language follows rules seems to put it outside the range of phenomena accessible to scientific investigation.

At this point a psycholinguist who wishes to preserve his standing as a natural scientist faces an old but always difficult decision. Should he withdraw and leave the study of language to others? Or should he give up all pretense of being a "natural scientist," searching for causal explanations, and embrace a more phenomenological approach? Or should he push blindly ahead with his empirical methods, hoping to find a causal basis for normative practices but running the risk that all his efforts will be wasted because rule-governed behavior in principle lies beyond the scope of natural science?

To withdraw means to abandon hope of understanding scientifically all those human mental processes that involve language in any important degree. To persevere means to face the enormously difficult, if not actually impossible, task of finding a place for normative rules in a descriptive science.

Difficult, yes. Still one wonders whether these alternatives are really as mutually exclusive as they have been made to seem.

The first thing we notice when we survey the languages of

the world is how few we can understand and how diverse they all seem. Not until one looks for some time does an even more significant observation emerge concerning the pervasive similarities in the midst of all this diversity.

Every human group that anthropologists have studied has spoken a language. The language always has a lexicon and a grammar. The lexicon is not a haphazard collection of vocalizations, but is highly organized; it always has pronouns, means for dealing with time, space, and number, words to represent true and false, the basic concepts necessary for propositional logic. The grammar has distinguishable levels of structure, some phonological, some syntactic. The phonology always contains both vowels and consonants, and the phonemes can always be described in terms of distinctive features drawn from a limited set of possibilities. The syntax always specifies rules for grouping elements sequentially into phrases and sentences, rules governing normal intonation, rules for transforming some types of sentences into other types.

The nature and importance of these common properties, called "linguistic universals," are only beginning to emerge as our knowledge of the world's languages grows more systematic.[10] These universals appear even in languages that developed with a minimum of interaction. One is forced to assume, therefore, either that (*a*) no other kind of linguistic practices are conceivable, or that (*b*) something in the biological makeup of human beings favors languages having these similarities. Only a moment's reflection is needed to reject (*a*). When one considers the variety of artificial languages developed in mathematics, in the communication sciences, in the use of computers, in symbolic logic, and elsewhere, it soon becomes apparent that the universal features of natural languages are not the only ones possible. Natural languages are, in fact, rather special and often seem unnecessarily complicated.

A popular belief regards human language as a more or less

free creation of the human intellect, as if its elements were chosen arbitrarily and could be combined into meaningful utterances by any rules that strike our collective fancy. The assumption is implicit, for example, in Wittgenstein's well-known conception of "the language game." This metaphor, which casts valuable light on many aspects of language, can if followed blindly lead one to think that all linguistic rules are just as arbitrary as, say, the rules of chess or football. As Lenneberg has pointed out, however, it makes a great deal of sense to inquire into the biological basis for language, but very little to ask about the biological foundations of card games.[11]

Man is the only animal to have a combinatorially productive language. In the jargon of biology, language is "a species-specific form of behavior." Other animals have signaling systems of various kinds and for various purposes—but only man has evolved this particular and highly improbable form of communication. Those who think of language as a free and spontaneous intellectual invention are also likely to believe that any animal with a brain sufficiently large to support a high level of intelligence can acquire a language. This assumption is demonstrably false. The human brain is not just an ape brain enlarged; its extra size is less important than its different structure. Moreover, Lenneberg has pointed out that nanocephalic dwarfs, with brains half the normal size but grown on the human blueprint, can use language reasonably well, and even mongoloids, not intelligent enough to perform the simplest functions for themselves, can acquire the rudiments.[12] Talking and understanding language do not depend on being intelligent or having a large brain. They depend on "being human."

Serious attempts have been made to teach animals to speak. If words were conditioned responses, animals as intelligent as chimpanzees or porpoises should be able to learn them. These attempts have uniformly failed in the past and, if the argument here is correct, they will always fail in the future—for just the same reason that attempts to teach fish to walk or dogs to fly would fail. Such efforts misconstrue the basis for our linguistic competence: they fly in the face of biological facts.*

Human language must be such that a child can acquire it. He acquires it, moreover, from parents who have no idea how to explain it to him. No careful schedule of rewards for correct or punishments for incorrect utterances is necessary. It is sufficient that the child be allowed to grow up naturally in an environment where language is used.

The child's achievement seems all the more remarkable when we recall the speed with which he accomplishes it and the limitations of his intelligence in other respects. It is difficult to avoid an impression that infants are little machines specially designed by nature to perform this particular learning task.

I believe this analogy with machines is worth pursuing. If we could imagine what a language-learning automaton would have to do, it would dramatize—and perhaps even clarify—what a child can do. The linguist and logician Noam Chomsky has argued that the description of such an automaton would comprise

---

* The belief that animals have, or could have, languages is as old as man's interest in the evolution of his special talent, but the truth of the matter has long been known. Listen, for example, to Max Müller (*Three Lectures on the Science of Language*) in 1889: "It is easy enough to show that animals communicate, but this is a fact which has never been doubted. Dogs who growl and bark leave no doubt in the minds of other dogs or cats, or even of man, of what they mean, but growling and barking are not language, nor do they even contain the elements of language."

Unfortunately, Müller's authority, great as it was, did not suffice, and in 1890 we hear Samuel Butler ("Thought and Language," in his *Collected Essays*) reply that although "growling and barking cannot be called very highly specialised language," still there is "a sayer, a sayee, and a covenanted symbol designedly applied. Our own speech is vertebrated and articulated by means of nouns, verbs, and the rules of grammar. A dog's speech is invertebrate, but I do not see how it is possible to deny that it possesses all the essential elements of language."

Müller and Butler did not argue about the facts of animal behavior which Darwin had described. Their disagreement arose more directly from differences of opinion about the correct definition of the term "language." Today our definitions of human language are more precise, so we can say with correspondingly more precision why Butler was wrong.

our hypothesis about the child's innate ability to learn languages or (to borrow a term from Ferdinand de Saussure) his innate *faculté de language*.[13]

Consider what information a language-learning automaton would be given to work with. Inputs to the machine would include a finite set of sentences, a finite set of nonsentences accompanied by some signal that they were incorrect, some way to indicate that one item is a repetition or elaboration or transformation of another, and some access to a universe of perceptual objects and events associated with the sentences. Inside the machine there would be a computer so programmed as to extract from these inputs the nature of the language, i.e., the particular syntactic rules by which sentences are generated, and the rules that associate with each syntactic structure a particular phonetic representation and semantic interpretation. The important question, of course, is what program of instructions would have to be given to the computer.

We could instruct the computer to discover any imaginable set of rules that might, in some formal sense of the term, constitute a grammar. This approach—the natural one if we believe that human languages can be infinitely diverse and various—is doomed from the start. The computer would have to evaluate an infinitude of possible grammars; with only a finite corpus of evidence it would be impossible, even if sufficient time were available for computation, to arrive at any unique solution.

A language-learning automaton could not possibly discover a suitable grammar unless some strong a priori assumptions were built into it from the start. These assumptions would limit the alternatives that the automaton considered—limit them presumably to the range defined by linguistic universals. The automaton would test various grammars of the appropriate form to see if they would generate all of the sentences and none of the nonsentences. Certain aspects would be tested before others; those found acceptable would be preserved for further evaluation. If we

The Psychology of Communication

wished the automaton to replicate a child's performance, the order in which these aspects would be evaluated could only be decided after careful analysis of the successive stages of language acquisition in human children.

The actual construction of such an automaton is, of course, far beyond our reach at the present time. That is not the point. The lesson to learn from such speculations is that the whole project would be impossible unless the automaton—and so, presumably, a child—knew in advance to look for particular kinds of regularities and correspondences, to discover rules of a rather special kind uniquely characteristic of human language in general.

The features that human infants are prepared to notice sharply limit the structure of any human language. Even if one imagines creating by decree a Newspeak in which this generalization were false, within one generation it would have become true again.

Psycholinguistics does not deal with social practices determined arbitrarily either by caprice or intelligent design, but with practices that grow organically out of the biological nature of man and the linguistic capacities of human infants. To that extent, at least, it is possible to define an area of empirical fact well within the reach of our scientific methods.

Another line of scientific investigation is opened up by the observation that we do not always follow our own rules. If this were not so, of course, we would not speak of rules, but of the laws of language. The fact that we make mistakes, and that we can know we made mistakes, is central to the psycholinguistic problem. Before we can see the empirical issue this entails, however, we should first draw a crucial distinction between theories of language and theories of the users of language.

There is nothing in the linguistic description of a language to indicate what mistakes will occur. Mistakes result from the psychological limitations of people who use the language, not from the language itself. It would be meaningless to state rules for making mistakes.

A formal characterization of a natural language in terms of a set of elements and rules for combining those elements must inevitably generate an infinitude of possible sentences that will never occur in actual use. Most of these sentences are too complicated for us. There is nothing mysterious about this. It is very similar to the situation in arithmetic where a student may understand perfectly the rules for multiplication, yet find that some multiplication problems are too difficult for him to do "in his head," i.e., without extending his memory capacity by the use of pencil and paper.

There is no longest grammatical sentence. There is no limit to the number of different grammatical sentences. Moreover, since the number of elements and rules is finite, there must be some rules and elements that can recur any number of times in a grammatical sentence. Chomsky has even managed to pinpoint a kind of recursive operation in language that, in principle, lies beyond the power of any finite device to perform indefinitely often. Compare these sentences:

(R) Remarkable is the rapidity of the motion of the wing of the hummingbird.
(L) The hummingbird's wing's motion's rapidity is remarkable.
(E) The rapidity that the motion that the wing that the hummingbird has has has is remarkable.

When you parse these sentences you find that the phrase structure of (R) dangles off to the right; each prepositional phrase hangs to the noun in the prepositional phrase preceding it. In (R), therefore, we see a type of recurring construction that has been called right-branching. Sentence (L), on the other hand, is left-branching; each possessive modifies the possessive immediately following. Finally, (E) is an onion; it grows by embedding sentences within sentences. Inside "The rapidity is remarkable" we first insert "the motion is rapid" by a syntactic transformation that permits us to construct relative clauses, and so we obtain "The rapidity that the motion has is remarkable." Then we repeat the transformation, this time inserting "the wing has motion" to obtain "The rapidity that the motion that the wing has has is remarkable." Repeating the transformation once more gives (E).

It is intuitively obvious that, of these three types of recursive operations, self-embedding (E) is psychologically the most difficult. Although they seem grammatical by any reasonable standard of grammar, such sentences never occur in ordinary usage because they exceed our cognitive capacities. Chomsky's achievement was to prove rigorously that any language that does *not* restrict this kind of recursive embedding contains sentences that cannot be spoken or understood by devices, human or mechanical, with finite memories. Any device that uses these rules must remember each left portion until it can be related to its corresponding right portion; if the memory of the user is limited, but the number of admissible left portions is not, it is inevitable that some admissible sentences will exceed the capacity of the user to process them correctly.[14]

It is necessary, therefore, to distinguish between a description of the language in terms of the rules that a person *knows* and uses and a description of that person's *performance* as a user of the rules. The distinction is sometimes criticized as "psycholatry" by strict adherents of behaviorism; "knowing" is considered too mentalistic and subjective, therefore unscientific. The objection cannot be taken seriously. Our conception of the rules that a language user knows is indeed a hypothetical construct, not something observed directly in his behavior. But if such hypotheses were to be forbidden, science in general would become an empty pursuit.

Given a reasonable hypothesis about the rules that a language user knows, the exploration of his limitations in following those rules is proper work for an experimental psychologist. "Psychology should assist us," a great linguist once said, "in understanding what is going on in the mind of speakers, and more particularly how they are led to deviate from previously existing rules in consequence of conflicting tendencies." Otto Jespersen made this request of psychology in 1924; now at last the work is beginning.[15]

One example. Stephen Isard and I[16] asked Harvard undergraduates to memorize several sentences that differed in degree of self-embedding. For instance, the twenty-two words in the right-branching sentence "we cheered the football squad that played the team that brought the mascot that chased the girls that were in the park" can be rearranged to give one, two, three, or four self-embeddings; with four it becomes, "The girls (that the mascot (that the team (that the football squad (that we cheered) played) brought) chased) were in the park." One self-embedding caused no difficulty; it was almost as easy to memorize as the sentence with none. Three or four embeddings were most difficult. When the sentence had two self-embeddings—"The team (that the football squad (that we cheered) played) brought the mascot that chased the girls that were in the park"—some subjects found it as easy to memorize as sentences with zero or one embedding, others found it as difficult as sentences with three or four. That is to say, everybody can manage one embedding, some people can manage two, but everybody has trouble with three or more.

Records of eye movements while people are reading such sentences show that the trouble begins with the long string of verbs, "cheered played brought," at which point all grasp of the sentence structure crumbles and they are left with a random list of verbs. This is just what would be expected from a computer executing a program that did not make provision for a sub-routine to refer to itself, i.e., that was not recursive. If our ability to handle this type of self-embedded recursion is really as limited as the experiment indicates, it places a strong limitation on the kinds of theories we can propose to explain our human capacities for processing information.

On the simpler levels of our psycholinguistic hierarchy the

The Psychology of Communication

pessimists are wrong; much remains there to be explored and systematized by scientific methods. How far these methods can carry us remains an open question. Although syntax seems well within our grasp and techniques for studying semantic systems are now beginning to emerge, understanding and belief raise problems well beyond the scope of linguistics. Perhaps it is there that scientific progress will be forced to halt.

No psychological process is more important or difficult to understand than understanding, and nowhere has scientific psychology proved more disappointing to those who have turned to it for help. The complaint is as old as scientific psychology itself. It was probably first seen clearly by Wilhelm Dilthey, who called for a new kind of psychology—a kind to which Karl Jaspers later gave the name *"verstehende Psychologie"*—and in one form or another the division has plagued psychologists ever since. Obviously a tremendous gulf separates the interpretation of a sentence from the understanding of a personality, a society, a historical epoch. But the gap is narrowing. Indeed, one can even pretend to see certain similarities between the generative theory of speech perception discussed above and the reconstructive intellectual processes that have been labeled *verstehende*. The analogy may some day prove helpful, but how optimistic one dares feel at the present time is not easily decided.

Meanwhile, the psycholinguists will undoubtedly continue to advance as far as they can. It should prove interesting to see how far that will be.

REFERENCES

1. A representative sample of research papers in this field can be found in S. Saporta, ed., *Psycholinguistics: A Book of Readings* (New York: Holt, Rinehart & Winston, 1962). R. Brown provides a highly readable survey from a psychologist's point of view in *Words and Things* (Glencoe, Ill.: The Free Press, 1957).

2. The CIBA Foundation Symposium, *Disorders of Language*

(London: J. & A. Churchill, 1964), provides an excellent sample of the current status of medical psycholinguistics.

3. P. L. Garvin, ed., *Natural Language and the Computer* (New York: McGraw-Hill, 1963).

4. My own opinions have been strongly influenced by Noam Chomsky. A rather technical exposition of this work can be found in Chapters 11–13 of R. D. Luce, R. R. Bush, and E. Galanter, eds., *Handbook of Mathematical Psychology* (New York: Wiley, 1963), from which many of the ideas discussed here have been drawn.

5. W. Epstein, "The Influence of Syntactical Structure on Learning," *American Journal of Psychology*, LXXIV (1961), 80–85.

6. G. A. Miller and S. Isard, "Some Perceptual Consequences of Linguistic Rules," *Journal of Verbal Learning and Verbal Behavior*, II (1963), 217–228. J. J. Katz and J. A. Fodor have recently contributed a thoughtful discussion of "The Structure of Semantic Theory," *Language*, XXXIX (1963), 170–210.

7. M. Halle and K. N. Stevens, "Speech Recognition: A Model and a Program for Research," *IRE Transactions of Information Theory*, IT–8 (1962), 155–159.

8. D. Bruce, "Effects of Context upon the Intelligibility of Heard Speech," in Colin Cherry, ed., *Information Theory* (London: Butterworths, 1956), pp. 245–252.

9. E. Lenneberg, "Understanding Language without Ability to Speak: A Case Report," *Journal of Abnormal and Social Psychology*, LXV (1962), 419–425.

10. J. Greenberg, ed., *Universals of Language* (Cambridge, Mass.: M.I.T. Technology Press, 1963).

11. E. Lenneberg, "Language, Evolution, and Purposive Behavior," in *Culture in History: Essays in Honor of Paul Radin* (New York: Columbia University Press, 1960).

12. E. Lenneberg, I. A. Nichols, and E. R. Rosenberger, "Primitive Stages of Language Development in Mongolism," in the *Proceedings of the 42nd Annual Meeting (1962) of the Association for Research in Nervous and Mental Diseases*.

13. N. Chomsky, "Explanatory Models in Linguistics," in E. Nagel, P. Suppes, and A. Tarski, eds., *Logic, Methodology, and Philosophy of Science* (Stanford: Stanford University Press, 1962), pp. 528–550.

14. N. Chomsky, *Syntactic Structures* (The Hague: Mouton, 1957).

15. O. Jespersen, *The Philosophy of Grammar* (London: Allen and Unwin, 1924), p. 344.

16. G. A. Miller and S. Isard, "Free Recall of Self-Embedded English Sentences," *Information and Control*, VII (1964), 292–303.

6

Computers, Communication, and Cognition

Some questions are like a cavity in a tooth: we keep coming back to probe them over and over until our tongues grow raw on their jagged edges. My present topic is one of these. It has been explored almost without intermission for three hundred years. No one could estimate how many learned essays and lectures have been devoted to it. I am sure everyone must have seen dozens of articles and books sharing the generic title *Minds, Machines, and Other Things,* and more are appearing daily. The pace at which these works are produced has grown in direct ratio to the complexity of the machines we can construct, which is to say that there has been an enormous outpouring of them in the last decade or two. The irritant for this recent outbreak of probing, of course, has been the emergence of automatic computing machines as a major influence in our lives. These new machines have enormously enlarged our conception of what a machine can be and do, and with every such enlargement it seems necessary to consider once again the ancient problem of the relation between men and machines.

Like most problems of any real importance, the relation between men and machines raises both theoretical and practical issues. The theoretical question—which is at least as old as the philosophy of Descartes—concerns the extent to which our brains can be considered as machines. The practical question—which is not entirely unrelated, but which, being practical, seems more immediately urgent—concerns the impact of these new machines on the social and economic institutions that regulate our daily coexistence.

Here I propose to discuss this topic on both levels: first, as a scientific psychologist whose main concern is to understand the human mind but who cannot keep from glancing over his shoulder occasionally to see if the machines are catching up; second, as a participant observer of the effect this new technology is having on our daily lives and future prospects. I shall consider the theoretical question first, because I think it has something to teach us that will be useful when we turn to more practical matters.

For many years I have studied the psychological processes that are entailed by our linguistic skills in communicating with one another, skills of enormous complexity and uniquely human in character. Since my interest in the psychological aspects of communication is even older than the automatic computers, I can remember what those days Before Computers were like. When I try to compare them with the present, I can think of no summary statement more appropriate than that made by a famous American athlete who said, "I've been rich, and I've been poor, and believe me, rich is better." Believe me, computers are better.

Lest I confuse you with the puzzle of what computers have to do with the psychology of communication, however, let me plunge *in medias res*.

CAN MACHINES THINK?

Several years ago the English mathematician A. M. Turing considered the difficult question of whether or not a computing machine can think. Since the semantic and metaphysical issues involved are apparently unresolvable, Turing rephrased it. Can a computing machine, he asked, behave in the way we behave when we say we are thinking? This rephrased question, he felt, might have an answer, and to make the issue perfectly definite, he proposed what he called the "imitation game." In the imitation game a computer is compared with a human being in terms of the answer it gives to an interrogator; if the interrogator is unable to determine when he is communicating with a human being and when he is communicating with a computer, then, Turing would say, the machine must be behaving in a human manner. And that, he implied, is all anyone should ever mean by the question, "Can machines think?" Turing, writing in 1950, predicted that within fifty years it would be possible to build and program computers that could do well at the imitation game. We have not seen them yet, but his prophecy has several years to run.

I have reminded you of Turing's question not because I wanted to approve or disapprove of it—certainly not because I thought I could answer it—but rather because it illustrates how intimate are the relations among computers, communication, and cognition. To understand better the cognitive processes we call thinking, Turing proposed to simulate them on a computing machine and to test the quality of the simulation in terms of the machine's performance in a communication situation. Human intelligence is best demonstrated when we communicate; if a machine is to be considered our equal, then it must communicate as we do. Which illustrates how such apparently unrelated topics as computers and communication can become important for psychologists.

Two easily recognizable groups frequently object when this question is seriously discussed. One group feels that such a question is morally reprehensible, that to compare man and machine diminishes the human spirit. Of course, science has been whittling away at our self-conceit ever since it pushed us out of the center of the universe and discovered the apes in our family tree, but whether science has thereby diminished or augmented human dignity is not entirely clear. In any case, these are not the critics I wish to answer. I respect their opinions; I hope they respond in kind.

In many ways the second group is more interesting, for it consists of men who know computers thoroughly, from top to bottom and inside out. Many of the real professionals—men who developed these wonderful machines and discovered how to use them—consider the question absolutely absurd. They understand all too well the limitations of their new toy and they would blush crimson if anyone caught them referring to it as a "giant brain" or a "thinking machine." They know whose brains did the real thinking behind all this new technology, and it was not the machine's.

I feel these objectors must be taken seriously, for they have earned their right to respect from those of us who hope to profit from the interaction of computers, communication, and cognition. The nature of their objections can be revealed most clearly, I believe, if we review briefly something of the history of their work.

THE AUTOMATIC DESK CALCULATOR

Leaving aside the well-known story of Charles Babbage and his Analytical Engines, the history of modern digital computers began about twenty-five or thirty years ago when engineers attempted to make the ordinary, manually operated desk calculator fully automatic.

Think for a moment of the way a human operator uses an adding machine. He begins with numerical data and a formula into which they are to be inserted. From the formula he sets up a sequence of operations that must be performed. Following this sequence, he pushes keys to put numbers into the machine, then pushes other keys to tell the machine what arithmetical operations to perform, and finally copies down the result on a piece of paper. These results can then be put back into the machine and further operations performed on them in turn, and the cycle repeated until the full list of instructions has been executed.

Key punching and copying are slow and tedious, so it is natural to think that the machine might just as well do them for itself. This was the idea behind the first "fully automatic" computers. The complete sequence of instructions was prepared in advance in a form the machine could sense and interpret; usually in the form of holes punched in a long paper tape. All the data were similarly prepared in advance on another tape. Then, instead of requiring the operator to copy down the intermediate results and feed them back into the machine, the machine was given a memory of its own—a sort of mechanical scratch pad—where numbers could be stored temporarily until they were needed. Once all was ready, the operator simply pressed a button and the whole computation ran off automatically. Not only did this enlarged adding machine eliminate most of the mistakes the human operators seem unable to avoid; it also worked much faster, so that computations previously considered too laborious to undertake by hand could now be accomplished in a few hours.

All this is a familiar story, of course. I mention it only to remind you of an attitude toward computers that prevailed in those days. Recall the use made of the early machines. One of the first projects was to compute the values of various important mathematical functions with great accuracy and to publish the resulting tables in order to make them available to scientists and mathematicians. No example could better illustrate how completely they missed the significance of their own invention. They

The Psychology of Communication

wanted to make it easier to perform accurate computations in the traditional sense of that term, and they knew from personal experience how valuable good mathematical tables had always been to a working mathematician. What they failed to see was that the computer itself made the mathematical tables unnecessary. From that time on nobody would bother to refer to a table when he could simply ask a computer to generate the value of the function as needed in the course of a computation. Now he wanted, not the tables, but the sequence of orders—the algorithm—for computing any value of the function.

It was, of course, the initial focus on numerical calculation that gave the new machines the name "computers." If that name had never been adopted, if we were suddenly faced for the first time with the modern machines and asked to find an appropriate name for them, I doubt that "computer" would now be our first choice. "Information-processing machines" would be more likely. Computing is only one of many operations a contemporary machine can perform, and some of its applications are wholly nonnumerical. But it was originally conceived as an extension and enlargement of the adding machine, so "computer" it has been ever since. When you look at computers as glorified adding machines, of course, there is little temptation to claim that they are thinking any more than their smaller ancestors had been thinking while their gears spun around.

THE AUTOMATIC FILING CABINET

Development did not stop there, however. If the first generation of computers can be said to have been modeled on the idea of the adding machine, the metaphor that is most appropriate for the second generation is the filing cabinet. I said that a certain amount of memory had been provided in the first machines, enough to enable them to store intermediate results temporarily during the process of computation. In the next stage this feature of the computer expanded enormously. All the skill and ingenuity of the inventors and machine designers was directed toward enlarging the capacity for storing information.

One consequence was to increase the speed at which machines could operate. To consult punched tapes every time a new datum or a new instruction is needed is relatively slow. With an enlarged memory, both data and instructions could be stored in the computer before the computations began, and could be retrieved with the speed of electrical conduction. As John von Neumann foresaw, storing the program of instructions in the machine turned out to be an especially significant advance, because a machine could then modify its own instructions as the computation proceeded and could select its next instruction from any point in the program depending on the outcome of preceding instructions. The flexibility of programing that resulted from this simple but profound innovation is an essential characteristic of modern digital machines.

Not only did larger memories make computation more efficient; they also made possible new applications for the machines in business and government. The contents of the filing cabinets—inventories, accounts, personnel records, and all varieties of economic and statistical information—could be dumped into the computer's enlarged memory, there to be processed by the fastest and most accurate bookkeeper ever created. And so it came to pass that the development of computers with large memories rewarded the customer and manufacturer alike. Without this financial support, the development of the new machines would never have been economically feasible.

The addition of a large memory, however, still did not turn a computing machine into a thinking machine. If a desk calculator does not think, and if a filing cabinet does not think, why should anyone imagine that they would start thinking when we put them together?

The Psychology of Communication

THE AUTOMATIC VOLTMETER

The third generation of computing machines also had a metaphorical progenitor: the voltmeter. The simplest kind of voltmeter has a pair of electrodes that serve as its sense organs to pick up differences in electrical potential, and some kind of scale-and-pointer arrangement to publish the measured voltage. When engineers began to dream about the possible embellishments they could add to this simple scheme, a whole sequence of new devices began to appear. First came the substitution of a cathode-ray oscilloscope for the scale and pointer. This resulted in an extremely useful instrument that converted electrical voltages into visible wave forms. A certain amount of electronic circuitry is needed to generate this visual display, of course, but not so much that it cannot be built into an easily portable cabinet. But as computers entered the scene it was inevitable that they would be used to process the incoming electrical data in ever more complicated ways before they were displayed. The result was the development of the most flexible and intricate "voltmeters" that the fertile engineering mind could imagine. This time economic support came from the military departments, because such systems are extremely valuable for processing information from radar receivers and other sources and presenting it in forms most convenient for military commanders.

For these computers the data do not have to be collected in advance and painstakingly copied in a form acceptable to the computer. These new machines have their own sense organs and can feed information directly into the computer, untouched by human hands, where it can be digested, processed, and displayed in a form more intelligible to a human operator. Their usefulness is not limited to military systems, of course. Wherever computations must be performed in what engineers like to call "real time," wherever an immediate display of the processed data is required, these super-voltmeters prove their value.

Take an adding machine, give it access to a filing cabinet, attach a battery of sensors to report events in the environment, throw in an oscilloscope or two for instantaneous communication with the operator, and you have a very modern computer. In some respects its general design resembles an organism's, which is the reason we use such terms as "memory" and "sense organs" to describe it. But those engineers who watched it grow, who know how much real human thinking is required to compose its instruction programs, are still not inclined to speak of it as a "thinking machine."

The machines are continuing to evolve, however, and perhaps they will become more humanoid as time goes on. For a glimpse of the future, we must look at current developments in new components and try to imagine how they may be put to use in the next generation of machines. I believe the most significant advances can be expected from the development of new and less expensive techniques for storing information.

THE NEXT STEP?

When Robert Graves delivered the annual Oration of the London School of Economics and Political Science, he approached his subject, as a poet should, by looking into the etymology of the word "money." *Money*, he found, came from the Latin *moneta*, which in turn was derived from the Greek *Mnemosyne*, meaning "an act of memory." Which only proves once again that the more things change, the more they are the same. This close association between money and memory has been forcefully reaffirmed in the modern world by the manufacturers of computers. I have been told that you could estimate the price of a computer in the United States rather accurately if you simply counted the number of binary digits that could be stored in its core memory as worth $1.00 apiece. A million bits of memory, a million-dollar computer. Obviously, if you need a very large computer, you must have a very large budget.

The Psychology of Communication

The cost of memory, measured in dollars per bit, has been decreasing steadily, however, and no doubt the figure I have just quoted is out of date by now. My friends who know about these things say that in a few years we should be able to produce storage devices for computers at a cost of only a fraction of a cent per bit. If so, an economic bottleneck will have been broken and fantastically large memories will become commercially available.

What new horizons will this open up? Predictions are always hazardous, but I believe it means that the next generation of machines will be modeled along the lines of what in the United States we call a public utility. Just as we can plug our electrical appliances into the wall and draw power from a central station, so in the future we shall be able to plug our typewriters into the telephone system and draw intelligence from a central computer.

Already a pilot model of such a system is operating at the Massachusetts Institute of Technology. Each subscriber has a teletypewriter beside his desk. When he wants to write a computer program, or consult data he has previously stored in the computer, or execute some particular computation, he simply turns on his typewriter and gives the appropriate instructions. The computer replies by writing the results on his typewriter, meanwhile keeping track of how much work it is doing so that he can be billed at the end of the month.

The trick that makes such systems possible with present-day computers is called "time sharing." The operator actually has access to the computer for only a small fraction of each second; the rest of the time the computer is working for its other customers. The computer operates so much faster than the customer that it can serve many other masters while the first is still thinking what to do next. The service is actually sequential and intermittent, but for most purposes it seems continuous to the men who are using it. With the very large memories that are soon to be available, the computer can become more than a filing cabinet; it can serve as a public archive where we can all store our data and our programs together.

The advantage of this public-service concept of computers is not merely that it saves a customer the inconvenience of walking from his office to the computer and standing in a queue to consult the oracle, although even that is not to be despised. More important is the intimate man-machine interaction that becomes possible. The great concealed cost of computers, as everyone knows who has tried to use them, lies in the time required to write programs of instructions for them. At present a program must be written, prepared for the computer, run, printed out, and the results studied to discover what mistakes must be corrected. This writing, running, studying, correcting cycle is slow and inefficient; a complete cycle usually takes twenty-four hours or longer. With a time-shared computer a programer can interact continuously with the machine and correct his mistakes as he goes along. The increase in efficiency resulting from this close man-machine collaboration has amazed even its most hopeful proponents. There is every reason to expect that convenience will foster similar efficiencies in other types of man-machine interaction.

Once, in Scotland, where they have not forgotten the lessons of the book of Genesis, I heard it said that a man is obviously superior to a woman because he has his wife to help him. I hope you will not consider me either profane or frivolous if, seeing giant computers almost at every scientist's elbow, I suggest that a man is obviously superior to a machine because he has his computer to help him. When they work so closely together they can make a powerful team.

The educated man in the street who reflects on recent advances in science and technology probably thinks first of jet airplanes, television sets, atomic bombs, or artificial earth satellites. Computers may come briefly to mind, but to most people a computer is a rather complicated, immobile box of hardware enshrined in some remote temple of mathematics, served by a few devoted priests trained to speak its mysterious, nonhuman language. Unless he has been personally initiated into one of the lower orders of this priesthood, he is not likely to appreciate the implications of the new computer technology. A computer is basically a tool, and tools have a way of seeming less important than the uses we put them to.

Those familiar with the course of events during the past ten or fifteen years, however, know that this particular tool has enormously accelerated the pace of science and technology. Those other miracles that seem more impressive to an ordinary citizen are all the product, in greater or lesser degree, of the increased intellectual power that computers have put at our disposal. I believe it is no exaggeration to say that the development of computers—modern, high-speed, stored-program, fully automatic digital computing machines—is probably the most significant thing that has happened in science during the past two decades. Within the next decade this wonderful tool should become immediately and continuously available to anyone with the need and the ability to use it.

GIANT BRAINS

Computers modeled after adding machines, filing cabinets, voltmeters—these are all well and good. But how long will it be before we have computers modeled after the human brain? When that day arrives even the most skeptical experts will be forced to reconsider their opinion of thinking machines. How close are we to accomplishing it?

Some believe we have already accomplished it. To balance the enthusiasts are the skeptics who believe we can never accomplish it. Let me say that it seems perfectly obvious to me that whatever else a brain may be it most certainly is *not* a digital computer. Until we begin to develop computers along entirely different lines than we have in the past, I see little hope of finding anything but crude analogies between them. We are today about as far from building a computer modeled on the human brain as

Archimedes was from building an atom bomb. I do not mean this as a criticism of computer engineers. I mean simply that we do not yet know enough about the brain or the principles on which it operates.

In the first blush of enthusiasm over the new machines we heard a great deal about analogies between relays and synapses, between electrical pulses and the nerve impulse, between the wiring of a computer and networks of neurons in the brain, etc. Some scientists still talk this way, but I believe that most people who have seriously compared the computer to the brain are more impressed by the differences than by the similarities.

You can build a computer along the lines of an adding machine or a filing cabinet or a voltmeter because these devices are relatively simple and because, since we invented them, we can understand them. The situation is quite different when we talk about building a computer modeled on the living brain. A brain is not some simple gadget that we conceived and built; it operates in ways still unknown to science or technology. Until its general principles are understood, it is vain to talk of building computers based on them. Let us therefore put aside the notion that there should be any point-for-point resemblance between computers and brains. We are not—or should not be—concerned with superficial analogies.

Which seems to put a full stop at the end of one line of speculation.

THE CYBERNETIC APPROACH

Why then should a psychologist, or any other student of living organisms, find computers interesting? And it is a fact that many of us do find them so. It is not merely because they process our data for us, or solve our equations for us, or control our experiments for us, although these services are all valuable. But our enthusiasm comes from a different source.

Someone has pointed out that a major difference between the physical and the biological sciences lies in the fact that the physical scientist formulates propositions of greater generality. A biologist is properly concerned only with organisms that actually exist. A physical scientist, however, is free to consider the set of all possible universes, of which our actual universe is only a special instance. This difference in method grows a bit hazy in the field of molecular biology, where biologists have adopted most effectively the strategy of the physical scientists, but at the level of whole, intact organisms adapting to their natural and social environments, I consider the difference both real and significant. Physicists deal generally with both the actual and the possible; biologists are largely confined to the realm of the actual.

Suppose, however, that we were to approach the study of whole organisms from a physical point of view. Suppose, that is, we were to study not merely the organisms that actually exist, but were to consider the full class of all possible systems—whether they exist or not, whether they are animate or inanimate—that might perform functions biological systems are known to perform. If this abstract approach were feasible, we might hope to formulate theories so universal and so powerful that they could be applied to organisms and machines alike. Then we would not be entangled in a fruitless argument that organisms are nothing but machines. Instead, both machines and organisms, insofar as they performed the same function, would be seen as particular instances of theoretical systems of far greater generality.

It is this possibility that provides the real source of our excitement, and keeps the cyberneticist hard at work in the face of all criticism that actual organisms and actual computing machines are very different things. He hopes to look beyond these actual instances to discover general principles governing all possible systems.

In order to adopt this abstract approach it is essential to select some clear and well-defined function as our starting point.

We must decide in advance what function we wish to generalize and then concentrate on defining and reproducing that aspect of behavior at the expense of all others. If, as in Turing's imitation game, we decide it is the function of linguistic communication we are going to generalize, then we will probably forget about the other functions—digestion, say, or driving an automobile—that people also perform. (Turing carried this abstraction even further; he was willing to let the interrogator communicate with his human and mechanical partners by teletypewriter, thus leaving out of account the problem of producing natural speech with all its intonations, hesitations, and subtle shadings.) Turing eliminated these other aspects of normal human behavior both to simplify and to clarify the problem; other aspects might be simulated as well, but the significantly human accomplishment that lies at the heart of his problem is our ability to string words together in meaningful, grammatical sentences. He abstracted one important and reasonably well-defined function that people perform and posed the problem of generalizing that particular function.

Our aim, therefore, is to enunciate general principles of the following form: "If any device is to perform function X, then that device is subject to or limited by the principles Y which must hold for all possible devices performing this function."

We want to formulate general principles that will describe all possible devices of a given class, regardless of their particular anatomy or mechanism.

Now with this aim in mind, consider one strategy we might adopt in our search for such general principles. It is obvious that machines have taken over many functions previously performed only by human beings. If we examine all the different ways in which machines have accomplished any one of these functions, we should find—since we understand the machines quite well—that they have certain features in common. If we can show that these common features are not the result of some poverty in their inventor's resources or imagination, but follow necessarily from the

The Psychology of Communication

nature of the function being performed, then we know that they must also apply to human beings insofar as human beings are also able to perform that function.

More often, however, we will find that our mechanical solutions fall into several distinct types, in which case we may be able to say that any device performing function X must be of type A, or type B, or type C, etc. Then we know that a human being, insofar as he also performs function X, must be of type A, B, or C, etc. We are then faced with a well-defined empirical problem. Can we determine which type a living organism is? At this point, an experimental scientist must undertake to devise tests that will settle the question.

Unfortunately, we are not always in the position of knowing that all devices performing a particular function *must* be of a single type, or *must* be one of a limited number of possible types. Even after we have invented three or four ways to perform the function, we may still be unable to show that we have exhausted all the possibilities. There may be other solutions that we have not been clever enough to see. This situation is far less satisfactory, but it is still worthwhile to try to determine whether or not living organisms belong to one of the general types that we have invented. If the answer is yes, then we understand that much more about the living organism; if the answer is no, then we are encouraged to continue our search for alternative ways of performing the function by machines. In either case, we know more than we did before.

These remarks on the virtues of abstraction have, I fear, been sufficiently abstract in themselves to try your patience. So let me resort to a few examples of this strategy of research.

AN EXAMPLE: NOISE

First, the case in which all devices performing function X must be of a single type. One example would be the following: any device that performs the function of a communication channel can produce only a finite number of distinguishably different output signals per second. Even in the best communication systems there is a residual level of noise that cannot be eliminated; as we try to make finer and finer distinctions between the output signals, we will eventually encounter this random noise, which sets a limit to the accuracy of our discriminations. This generalization must hold for human beings as well, insofar as human beings can perform the function of a communication channel. Offhand, this principle is so general that there would seem to be little for an experimental scientist to do about it. In fact, however, it has led to a great deal of experimentation by psychologists, who have wanted to measure the noise level of the human channel. The measurement is generally stated in units called "bits" of information. It has been estimated that, under optimal conditions, a human being has a channel capacity of about twenty-five bits per second. This means that each second a human channel can select any one from about 2^{25} = two hundred million distinguishably different responses. This may impress you as a very large number, but before you begin to feel too proud of yourselves, let me remind you that our electronic communication channels regularly transmit thousands or millions of bits of information per second. By comparison, our capacity of twenty-five bits per second is puny indeed. Considered as communication channels, human beings have a rather high noise level.

I would like to call your attention to the exact wording I have used. I said that this general law must hold for human beings *insofar as human beings perform the particular function* in question. What I have *not* said is that, since the laws governing communication channels can be applied to human beings, human beings are nothing but communication channels. If you intend to explore further into this suburb of science, you should mark this difference well. Always distrust the man who tells you that human beings are "nothing but" something else, for he is deliberately concealing from you the abstraction on which his claim is based. Human beings are nothing but human beings.

AN EXAMPLE: SUBROUTINES

Next, the case in which all devices performing function X must belong to one of a limited set of possible types. Let us begin with a simple example.

Consider the following: any device that is to perform the function of answering a question must either (*a*) obtain the answer by consulting some memory where the answer is stored, or (*b*) synthesize the answer from other information according to a set of rules. If, for example, you are asked the value of the logarithm of 75, you can either (*a*) remember it—which would include looking it up in a table that remembered it for you—or (*b*) compute it by carrying out some rather tedious calculation that most of us do not remember how to do. Similarly, if in the course of solving some problem on a computer it will be necessary to know the value of a logarithm, we must either store a table of logarithms in the computer's memory in advance, or we must give the computer a sequence of instructions that will enable it to calculate the value when it is needed. With a computer, alternative (*b*) would generally be preferred, since it uses the memory more efficiently, and we would prepare what is called a "subroutine" for computing logarithms. Each time the value of a logarithm was needed in the course of executing the main routine, the computer would interrupt what it was doing, refer to the logarithm subroutine to calculate the answer, and then resume the main routine where it had been left off.

In most cases both techniques are employed; some information is stored in memory, other information is reconstructed as needed. A fascinating problem for a psychologist is to try to tease apart these two methods of producing answers in human beings. The question has to be asked about each area of information separately, but it is my strong impression that we, like the computer, make very extensive use of the reconstructive method, that we remember most things by following rules for deducing what we need to know from other facts. We are, in short, equipped with a large assortment of subroutines—using that term now in a broad sense—that we can use to generate answers as they are needed.

AN EXAMPLE: RECURSIVE SUBROUTINES

For a more esoteric illustration, let me refer to some of my own reserach. The idea behind it came from a comparison of the structure of computer programs and the structure of grammatical sentences, so I must introduce it with a few remarks about the way such structures are put together.

Once we have reached the level of complexity in programing computers where we can have subroutines stored away for use as needed, an interesting possibility emerges. Ordinarily, we interrupt the main routine to perform the subroutine, then return to the main routine when the subroutine is finished. It is possible, however, for one subroutine to refer to another subroutine. That is to say, we can program a computer in such a way that the subroutine itself is interrupted while some other subroutine is executed; when this second subroutine is completed, the computer returns to the first subroutine again, and when it in turn is finished, goes back to the main routine. The interruption is itself interrupted. Any busy person will recognize how easily this can happen.

An interesting situation arises when we ask whether or not a subroutine can refer to itself. Consider what this would mean. The computer interrupts its main routine to go into subroutine S. In the middle of executing subroutine S, however, before S is finished, the computer is instructed to stop what it is doing and execute subroutine S. This may sound a bit complicated, perhaps, but actually it is not. No trouble will arise until subroutine S is completed and the computer must decide where to resume its work. Unless special precautions are taken in writing the program the

The Psychology of Communication

computer will not be able to remember that the first time it finishes subroutine S it must re-enter subroutine S, and the second time it finishes subroutine S it must return to the main routine. In the slang of computer programers, the second re-entry address is likely to "clobber" the machine's memory of the original re-entry address. The situation gets even more tangled, of course, if subroutine S can call on itself repeatedly, for each time it does so a new re-entry address must be remembered.

Programs that are written in such a way that subroutines can refer to themselves repeatedly in mid-flight are generally called "recursive," and programs that do not make such provisions are called "nonrecursive." This gives us our two possible types of programs, or, if you like, two possible types of systems. It turns out, for reasons I will not go into, that recursive systems are intrinsically more powerful than nonrecursive systems; they can do everything a nonrecursive system can do, plus some other things that are impossible for the nonrecursive system. So the distinction I have described, although it may seem rather subtle, is very important. Recursiveness is a desirable property to have in a computer programing language, and many ingenious stratagems have been devised to make it available.

Now, enter the psychologist, armed with a conviction that people use subroutines in their own cognitive operations. His question is obvious. Since any device that consults subroutines is either recursive or nonrecursive, and since people use subroutines, which type of device are they?

One way to investigate this question presents itself in the realm of language. It is a feature of natural language—by "natural language" I mean the languages we ordinarily use in speaking to one another, as opposed to the "artificial language" that we have developed for mathematics, logic, computer programing, and so on—it is a feature of natural languages that sentences can be inserted inside of sentences. For example, "The king who said, 'My kingdom for a horse,' is dead" contains the sentence, "My kingdom for a horse" embedded in the middle of another sentence, "The king is dead."

Think of a listener as processing information in order to understand this sentence. Obviously, his analysis of one sentence must be interrupted while he analyzes the embedded sentence. When he finishes analyzing the embedded sentence, he must then resume his analysis of the original sentence. Here we have all the elements present in a computer subroutine.

The question, of course, is whether we can do this more than once, that is to say, recursively. Let us try: "The person who cited, 'The king who said, "My kingdom for a horse," is dead,' as an example is a psychologist." Most people find this just on the borderline of intelligibility: if I had not prepared you for it, you probably would not have understood. Let us go one step more: "The audience who just heard, 'The person who cited, "The king who said, 'My kingdom for a horse,' is dead," as an example is a psychologist,' is very patient." By now you should be ready to give up. If not, of course, I could go on this way indefinitely.

A PSYCHOLOGICAL EXPERIMENT

Even though they are grammatical, such sentences are obviously difficult to understand, which suggests that our ability to use subroutines that refer to themselves must be rather limited. My colleagues and I, however, wished to make a more objective measurement, so we asked people—students at Harvard University—to memorize sentences with various amounts of self-embedding in them. The grammatical device we used to embed sentences inside of sentences was the relative clause, which is particularly convenient because all the sentences can have the same length.

Let me build up one example for you. Begin with the following five sentences: "The movie was applauded by the critics," "The script made the movie," "The novel became the script," "The producer discovered the novel," and "She thanked the producer."

The Psychology of Communication

The most intelligible way to combine these five sentences into one involves no embedding at all:

"She thanked the producer who discovered the novel that became the script that made the movie that was applauded by the critics."

There is nothing difficult here. The structure of this sentence is the same as the nursery rhyme, "This is the cow with the crumpled horn that tossed the dog that worried the cat that killed the rat that ate the malt that lay in the house that Jack built." And that, of course, is easily understood and enjoyed by young children.

Now let us embed one of these relative clauses:

"The producer (whom she thanked) discovered the novel that became the script that made the movie that was applauded by the critics."

There are still no problems. Everyone who knows English can drop into a subroutine for analyzing one embedded relative clause.

The interesting situation arises when we insert another relative clause into the middle of the first one, as follows:

"The novel (that the producer (whom she thanked) discovered) became the script that made the movie that was applauded by the critics."

Now the plot begins to thicken, and it gets even thicker when we do it once more:

"The script (that the novel (that the producer (whom she thanked) discovered) became) made the movie that was applauded by the critics."

Finally, with four embeddings:

"The movie (that the script (that the novel (that the producer (whom she thanked) discovered) became) made) was applauded by the critics."

If you are able to understand this final version, it is only because I led you into it gradually. Our students did not have such a gentle initiation. They would hear for the first time something like:

"The story that the book that the man whom the girl that Jack kissed met wrote told was about a nuclear war."

Their task was to memorize it, and we measured how well they could remember it as a function of the amount of studying they had done. Every version of the sentence contained exactly the same twenty-two words. All we did was to rearrange their order a bit, and so rearranged the order in which the listener's cognitive operations of analysis had to be performed. In spite of their unusual appearance, however, all of these embedded sentences are perfectly grammatical, by any reasonable interpretation of English grammar.

I think you can predict from your own reactions the performance of the subjects in our experiment. The simplest way to summarize the results is to say that everyone could handle one embedded clause, some could handle two, but everyone had trouble with three or more. The ability of some people to handle two embeddings indicates that we are not entirely bereft of recursive facilities, but their inability to deal easily with three or more tells us that our recursive resources, whatever they may be, are extremely limited, even in subjects as intelligent as Harvard students are reputed to be.

Introspection—that unreliable but irresistibly convenient tool of the psychologist—indicates that all is proceeding quite well with the embedded sentence until we encounter the long string of predicates, ". . . thanked discovered became made was applauded . . . ," at which point our grasp of sentence structure collapses and we are left with a haphazard string of verbs. We are unable to locate the subjects associated with each successive predicate; that, of course, is exactly what we would predict if people were analyzing them as would a nonrecursive computing machine that could not remember its re-entry addresses. This subjective impression has been tested objectively by studying eye move-

The Psychology of Communication

ments as people try to read such embedded sentences. Their eyes move forward along the line in a normal fashion until they come to the third or fourth verb; at that point, regressive eye movements occur as they begin to look frantically back and forth for the subject associated with each verb.

Now, I would be the last to claim that this little experiment solves all the problems of psychology, but I do think it is amusing and that it establishes an important point, namely, that we are very poor at dealing with recursive interruptions. If this result is confirmed in studies of interruption in other kinds of tasks, we may have to assign human beings to the general category of non-recursive devices. The fact that we are able to process information as effectively as we do without this powerful tool makes our cognitive functions all the more fascinating as objects for scientific research.

It is true that in everyday affairs we do not seem to suffer too severely from this limitation. But if you will recall the everyday situations in which you were able to resume what you were doing after your interruptions had been interrupted, I think you will agree that you were able to resume because the interrupted task itself remembered for you. If you are interrupted while painting a wall, when you return the wall will provide an unmistakable reminder of how far you had gone and where you should resume. It is only when you cannot count on the environment to remember your re-entry point that your cognitive limitations become a handicap. Perhaps it is because we can usually count on the task to remember for us that we have not evolved more extensive powers for recursion.

When we know that living organisms must, insofar as they are able to perform function X, fall into one of a limited set of types of devices for performing that task, we are in a relatively good position to learn something interesting about them. In most situations, however, the most we can say is that there are several different ways a machine might perform the function, and all we can ask is whether the organism performs it similarly. If the organism does not—which will usually be the case unless we are very lucky—there is little we can do but continue to study the problem. There are so many examples of this sort, each surrounded by its own special penumbra of ignorance, that I dare not launch into examples.

IMPLICATIONS FOR THE FUTURE

If I seem to have wandered off into rather specific examples and to have lost the main thread of my message, you must forgive me. Even so, however, I have not completely wasted your time if these examples have managed to convey some sense of the detail with which a function must be analyzed before we can begin to talk of performing it with a computing machine. Learning to cope with the extreme literalness of computers is good discipline for a psychological theorist, for many of us are inclined to rely implicitly on common-sense explanations that tempt us to think we understand a process when, in fact, we cannot describe any detailed operations by which it might be accomplished.

As we have begun to spell out in detail what these cognitive operations might be, we have begun to see that above—or perhaps behind—the mass of detail there are often very general principles that govern the operation of any device, living or nonliving, capable of performing the function in question. It is not a matter of reducing men to machines, but of discovering general principles applicable to men and machines alike. And this is the exciting prospect that I wished to display for your consideration.

Practical applications of this kind of knowledge are difficult to foresee with either confidence or clarity, but I believe I can point to one general consequence that will emerge as our knowledge of information processing systems increases. By classifying man ever more accurately with respect to his capacities and incapacities for processing information, by discovering more about the general system that he exemplifies, we will gain increasingly deeper insight into how best to use computers to perform functions that are difficult for him. As our understanding increases, I think we will be better able to optimize the man-machine team. Mechanical intelligence will not ultimately replace human intelligence, but rather, by complementing our human intelligence, will supplement and amplify it. We will learn to supply by mechanical organs those functions that natural evolution has failed to provide.

Those of us who are optimistic about this general strategy of research expect that it will prove valuable in all areas of the biological, psychological, and social sciences. Perhaps we should restrain our enthusiasm until we have more substantial accomplishments to report. But if these advances actually occur, they will undoubtedly have rather profound effects on our lives as ordinary citizens, effects that may entail major readjustment in our conception of ourselves and our social institutions. If such adjustments do lie ahead, as a consequence of our advancing knowledge of information-processing systems, it would be criminally negligent of scientists not to discuss them as publicly as possible.

WILL OUR COMPUTERS DESTROY US?

I said that I would discuss the ancient problem of the relation between men and machines on two levels. So far I have done so in a semiphilosophical vein; I have argued that the old question as to whether men are nothing but machines should be replaced by a more broadly conceived question about the nature of possible systems that both men and machines might exemplify as actual instances. There is, however, another and more practical question about the relation between men and machines, a question that has been growing increasingly urgent as the new machines have begun to shape the next step forward in our industrial revolution. I would be remiss if, in my academic concentration, I pretended that this more aggravating aspect of our mechanical marvels did not exist. In closing, I would like to say just a few words about the human problems we face in adapting ourselves and our society to the new world ahead of us.

We have recently heard a great deal about the disruptive effects of computing machines on our social and economic institutions. In industry, computers mean automation, and automation is supposed to mean unemployment. The United States, with its extravagant investment in computers, is plagued by unemployment for unskilled workers; it is frequently argued that these facts are causally related. Already the computers have begun to displace workers whose tasks are simple and repetitive: clerical workers, workers on assembly lines, and the like. The variety of jobs formerly done only by humans that the machine can perform more rapidly, accurately, and economically increases with each new generation of computers. If we extrapolate this trend, say the pessimists, we are faced with the prospect of mass unemployment for all but a handful of highly trained, highly intelligent professionals, who will then be even more influential and overworked than they are at present. Only recently a distinguished English physicist predicted that within twenty years electronic engineers might have to become conscientious objectors in order to prevent these pernicious machines from wrecking our social and economic institutions.

According to the prophets of doom, our situation is hopeless. The computer is already stirring up industrial strife as management desires and labor resists the effects of automation. Great masses of people will soon be unemployed, and the devil will surely find work for their idle hands. The gap between advanced and developing nations will increase, thus heightening international tensions. People will become demoralized when the personal identification and self-respect that work confers is suddenly withdrawn. The educational system will be unable to educate citizens for life in the Leisure State. All the industrial and commercial

The Psychology of Communication

machinery of production and distribution of commodities will have to be taken over by the state, which will lead inevitably to tighter economic controls or even dictatorship. And so on and on runs this hopeless catalogue. I find it difficult to state these awful anticipations convincingly, because I do not believe in them, but those who do believe can make Aldous Huxley's *Brave New World* and George Orwell's *1984* sound like optimistic promises of salvation. Little wonder that some have thrown up their hands in dismay and proposed that we must somehow find a way to stop, or at least slow, the pace of this technological nightmare.

What can we do about it? It is foolish to dream of reversing history. We cannot pass laws forbidding science and technology. The computing machines are here, and they will not merely stay; they will group bigger, faster, and more useful every year. They will grow because engineers want to build them, scientists want to use them, industrialists want to employ them, soldiers want to enlist them in new weapons systems, politicians want their help in the processes of government. In short, they will flourish because they enable us to accomplish tasks that could never before have been undertaken, no matter how many un-skilled laborers we might have set to work. Computers will continue to amplify our intelligence for just the same reason that engines continue to amplify our muscles. The question we must ask is not whether we shall have computers or not have com-puters, but rather, since we are going to have them, how can we make the most humane and intelligent use of them?

THE CASE FOR OPTIMISM

Fear of future technology seems to derive from two assump-tions, both of which are highly dubious, if not demonstrably false. These assumptions are, first, that the amount of work to be done in the future is finite, and, second, that anything men can do, ma-chines can do better.

Computers, Communication, and Cognition

Concerning the first, the argument of despair goes as follows. Automation means that long years of performing a job manually are sacrificed for a smaller amount of work required now to build a machine that will do the long-term job automatically. Doing future work now may give a present boost to some sectors of the economy, but it is feared that this boost will quickly spend itself and future generations will be left with nothing to do. This fear of future unemployment arising from the present construction of machines is far older than the Age of Computers. The Emperor Vespasian is said to have rejected a proposal for a hoisting machine because he had to keep his poor employed. But the argument was bad in Vespasian's day, and it has not improved with age.

If the total amount of future work to be done were limited, there might be some plausibility to this argument; future work, being limited, should be left for future generations to do. But there is little reason to believe that this is true. The amount of work involved merely in achieving full automation of industry is enormous, and no one who can contribute to it will need to go unemployed for centuries to come. Moreover, this enterprise will almost certainly be supplemented by the further development of new products and new technologies.

Automation does not mean future unemployment. What it *does* mean, however, is a redistribution of our working force into new occupations, with all the attendant social stress that such shifts always generate. The demands that this shift will place on our educational system are, of course, staggering—but not impossible to meet if we foresee them and begin to plan for them immediately.

The second basis for anxiety—that machines can do anything better than men—is equally unrealistic. It rests on the assumption that there is no real difference between human intelligence and mechanical intelligence, so that as the level of mechanical intelligence increases all but the most highly intelligent elite among human beings will find themselves redundant.

To calm such fears, we should remember first that computers are expensive. Given the economic realities that are likely to be with us for some time to come, a mechanical slave cannot be considered "better" than a human employee unless it can do the job equally well at a lower total cost. This condition will often be a difficult one to satisfy. Many labor-saving devices already exist that we do not use because they are not economically feasible. Even if you bite the mechanistic bullet and grant that men are nothing but machines, still you must admit that they are very clever computing machines indeed, and that we know a great deal about how to manufacture and maintain them. They will remain economically competitive with their glass-and-metal rivals for a long time to come, if not indefinitely.

At present the machines are best at those highly routine operations and decisions that must be performed repeatedly according to explicit rules and criteria—usually the kind of jobs that are brutalizing for men to do anyway. But not all our work has this routine, repetitive character, and there is some hope that machines may be able in the future to perform more subtle kinds of intellectual work. Even if this should prove to be the case, all the evidence suggests that it will not be economically realistic for them to replace humans at it on a large scale. For example, who would be willing to spend millions creating a mechanical executive when they can hire a human executive for a few thousand a year? This situation is not limited to executive functions, of course, but applies to most of the interesting kinds of work that human beings can do. The fact that it might conceivably be possible to replace men by machines does not say anything about where it will prove economical to do so.

Moreover, let me repeat that as yet I see little reason to believe that machines *can* do everything that men can do. I have already tried to say how different actual computing machines and actual brains really are. What this difference means is that there are some things that the machines do better than we, and other things that we do better than they. I have even argued that cybernetics is less concerned to show that brains are machines than to show that both brains and machines must follow some very general principles applicable to all information-processing systems, whatever their construction or mode of operation may be. In the future we will become increasingly better able—on the basis of our increasing understanding of what men can and cannot do—to use machines to supplement our own competencies. Surely this prospect is nothing to inspire dread or despair. In my private catalogue of absurdities I put the man who fears the mechanical aids of the future along with the teacher who fears the printing press because its books may put him out of business. If it is possible to spare ourselves onerous mechanical chores, we will be just that much freer to do those things that only human beings can do, or want to do. I expect that the division of labor between men and machines, described in the most general terms, will ultimately correspond to a division between finding problems and solving them, but exactly what I mean by that distinction is not yet clear, even to me.

I am, as you can see, an optimist about the future course of the industrial revolution. I do not grant that the introduction of computing machines has changed the larger historical trend of technological progress, or that we are any less able to cope with the consequences of this new advance than we have been able to cope with the inventions of the past. Please do not mistake my optimism for blindness to the very real problems that we will face. All our imagination and good will will be needed to ensure that these new machines serve the public interest, and to modify our social, economic, and educational institutions to harmonize with a future that we all know is coming.

We have talked for three hundred years about the relation between men and machines. At first it was just philosophical speculation. As the gap between men and machines has narrowed— not by degrading man, let me repeat, but by enriching our con-

The Psychology of Communication

ception of a machine—the question has moved from the philosopher's study through the scientist's laboratory and the industrialist's factory and on to the desks of our national planners. This progression has become a familiar one in recent times as more and more of our abstract ideas are converted into hard realities. Each new social problem that results seems more baffling and more difficult than the one before. But I have faith that our national planners will once again be able to rise to the occasion. After all, this time they will have their computers to help them.

7

Project Grammarama

The interrogative mode is one of civilized man's most effective tactics for putting the other fellow on the defensive. Some questions don't, of course, but many do; their classification would provide suitable diversion for some quiet cocktail hour. There would be the contemptuous, so-what question; the negative question that implies its own answer; the teasing, you-mean-you-didn't-know question; the angry, what-are-you-doing question; etc. Personally, I am most vulnerable to the discouraging, why-would-anybody question. I usually interpret it to mean that the questioner believes I couldn't possibly have known what I was doing. It is most annoying when I possibly didn't.

The Psychology of Communication

Why would anybody undertake Project Grammarama?

Several years ago a friend of mine was invited to lecture to a colloquium of fellow scientists and their students at another university. Mindful of the honor, he prepared a closely reasoned account of his research, summarizing precisely and powerfully the results of several years' labor. When he told me about it later he confessed that he just might have been so very precise, powerful, and closely reasoned as to overtax somewhat the unaided ear. In any case, he read his paper in a loud, clear voice for one hour until he reached the end.

The chairman of the colloquium rose and asked whether there were any comments or questions. There was a silent, embarrassed pause. The chairman waited. The speaker waited, his eye on the chairman. Finally, from the rear of the room, "Please, sir," asked a confused but courageous auditor, "why would anybody want to do that research?"

In such situations complete honesty is the only defense. "I did it," my friend said, "because nobody asked me to manage the Red Sox."

Why did I undertake grammarama? It is not so much fun as baseball, perhaps. More like detective stories or crossword puzzles. If something comes of it I will surely be crowned a king in Serendip.

Is it risky to admit publicly that your work is fun? (It seems insufficiently dignified.) I chance it in order to say that grammarama is a sort of intellectual hobby for me, as much a source of interesting questions as of satisfying answers. Metaphorically, I would characterize Project Grammarama as a pleasant field trip through some rather exotic psycholinguistic meadows; I have collected a few specimens that look interesting, but so far not much has been accomplished by way of taxonomy. In more literal terms, it is a program of laboratory experiments to investigate how people learn the grammatical rules underlying artificial languages. But I prefer to think of it as an intellectual field trip.

It began at Stanford University during the summer of 1957 when Noam Chomsky and I collaborated on a study of algebraic systems that at the time he called "finite state grammars." The fruit of our summer's work was two papers. One, which summarized rather more completely than necessary almost everything you might care to know about the formal properties of finite state grammars, was subsequently published.[7] The second, which contained the seeds of grammarama, was not. We presented the second paper[16] to a conference at the University of Michigan at the end of the summer. The conference dealt with pattern perception; our paper, which concerned certain inductive procedures for discovering formal properties of artificial linguistic systems, was entitled "Pattern Conception"—conception being substituted in our title because the patterns we were interested in seemed too abstract to be truly perceptual.

The proceedings of the Michigan conference were to be published, and our manuscript was duly deposited with the chairman. Many years have now passed and, so far as I know, the proceedings have never seen the light of day. That may have been a good thing. I have since lost all my copies, which may also have been a good thing. But our effort was not entirely wasted. Somewhere R. J. Solomonoff [28, 29, 30] saw the paper and set about solving our problem properly.

The problem went like this. Imagine a system that has a finite number of distinguishably different internal states that it can get into. Select one of those states as the "start" and one as the "finish." The system operates by moving from one state to another. Each shift of state can be accompanied by the emission of a signal chosen from a finite set of possible signals characteristic of the particular antecedent state. As the system chugs ahead, it gives off a steady string of such signals. Not just any sequence can occur, of course. What can occur at any given point in the string depends on the state the system is in and the possible signals available in that state; the set of possible signals changes as the system

The Psychology of Communication

changes states. Whenever the system begins in the starting state and works away steadily producing signals until it reaches the end state, that string of signals is said to be "well formed," or, if you are thinking linguistically (as Chomsky and I were), "grammatical." The set of grammatical strings it can produce is the language generated by that grammar. All this and more was the basis for our first paper, published in 1958.

Let me resort to contemporary fiction for a more concrete picture of these ideas in linguistic action. In his novel *The Tin Men*,[9] Michael Frayn had an opportunity to consider the automation of newspaper writing. Goldwasser, the hero, sometimes took himself out of himself by pretending to be a computer and going through one of a set of cards, observing the same logical rules and making the same random choices that a computer would observe in order to compose a newspaper story from them. One of Goldwasser's favorites was "the set of instructions for composing a news story on a royal occasion."

Goldwasser would open the filing cabinet and pick out the first card in the set. *Traditionally,* it read. Next there was a random choice to be made among *coronations, engagements, funerals, weddings, comings of age, births, deaths,* or *the churching of women.* If he picked *funerals,* he would be directed on to a card reading with simple perfection *are occasions for mourning;* when he closed his eyes and drew *weddings,* he was sent on to *are occasions for rejoicing. The wedding of X and Y* followed in logical sequence and brought him to a choice between *is no exception* and *is a case in point.* Either way there followed *indeed.* Indeed, whichever occasion he started with, whether weddings, coronations, deaths, or births, he always reached this same elegant bottleneck. Goldwasser then drew in quick succession *it is a particularly happy occasion, rarely,* and *can there have been a more popular couple.* From the next selection he drew *X has won himself/herself a special place in the nation's affections,* which forced him to go on to *and the British people have clearly taken Y to their hearts already.* Goldwasser was momentarily surprised and a little disturbed to realize that the word "fitting" had still not come up, but he drew it on the next card—*it is especially fitting that.* This gave him *the bride/bridegroom should be,* and an open choice between *of such a noble and illustrious line, a commoner in these democratic times, from a nation with which this country has long enjoyed a particularly close and cordial relationship,* and *from a nation with which this country's relations have not in the past been always happy.* So Goldwasser proceeded on and on, weaving clichés into newspaper stories. He felt confident that with just a few improvements the whole business of writing newspapers could be turned over to computing machines.

Each choice point corresponds to what I have called a state of the system. Each successive decision adds a cliché to the story and moves the generator along to another state, where it faces another choice. Frayn's heroes—both Goldwasser and the computer—followed the rules of a finite state grammar.

Out of such games came grammarama. Goldwasser's game, which uses meaningful words and phrases, is a special case; its humor is that the essential meaninglessness of the performance is so transparently concealed. Grammarama makes no attempt at concealment. Suppose that someone is shown arbitrary strings of signals and allowed to ask which are grammatical and which are not. Suppose moreover that the rules of our game do *not* resemble English grammar, and that the signals are *not* familiar English words and phrases. In this more general form there is no limit to the variety of artificial grammars we could invent. Imagine, in short, a completely novel, completely abstract grammar and meaningless vocabulary. With nothing more than that—with no meanings, no sensible use of the strings, with nothing but formal criteria as a guide—can a person discover the grammatical rules underlying the language? And if so, what is the best way for him to go at it?

In the paper we read at the Michigan conference Chomsky

The Psychology of Communication

and I simply posed this question and suggested one strategy that a person might follow in order to solve the problem—to the extent that an inductive problem can be solved after a finite number of observations. Solomonoff carried his strategic speculations much further than we, so it matters little that I can no longer remember the theoretical suggestions we made at that time.

However, I think a more interesting question is the empirical one. Suppose you actually gave people this kind of abstract problem. Instead of trying to devise some optimal strategy that they ought to follow, suppose you put people into this situation and watched what they actually did. What kinds of problem-solving strategies would they hit on? That empirical question was the beginning of Project Grammarama. From the very first it had about it an atmosphere of intellectual fun and games. Also from the very first the results have had a slippery way of avoiding publication.

If you need something more definite to visualize when you think of finite state grammars (or, as we call them now, "regular grammars"), an analogy with a road map may help. The internal states are cities, represented on the map by small circles. The cities are connected by lines for the (one-way) roads, which represent possible transitions. Each road is associated with a signal. One city is where I live, another is where I am going. I set out blindly to get there. Every time I travel down some road from one city to the next I write down the signal associated with the road I have just traveled. Eventually, when I get to my destination, I will have produced a string of signals representing the path I took. In the linguistic interpretation, each permissible path between those two cities corresponds to a "sentence." The set of all possible paths corresponds to the "language" of that road-map "grammar."

Figure 10 is an example of a grammatical road map. The signals are single letters of the alphabet. If we start in state 0, we have a choice between path N and path S. If we choose S, we go to state 3, where now we have a choice between X and S. X leaves

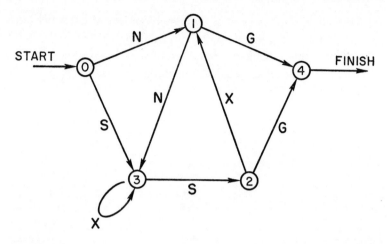

FIGURE 10. A "road map" representing a regular grammar. Any string of letters that is produced along a path starting in state 0 and finishing in state 4 is said to be grammatical.

us still in state 3, but S takes us on to state 2, etc. A list of all the paths from start to finish, ordered from shortest to longest, would begin

> NG
> SSG
> NNSG
> SSXG
> SXSG
> NNSXG
> NNXSG
> SXSXG
> SXXSG
> etc.

and it would go on forever, because there is no longest path. Seen in this way, a grammar is a set of rules for *producing* grammatical sequences.

A grammar can also be viewed as a set of rules for *selecting* grammatical sequences from the infinite variety of letter permutations that are conceivable with a given alphabet of signals. Imagine that all the possible permutations of signals have been ordered for length and alphabetized. If the alphabet is, say, N,G,S, and X, then the list of all possible strings would be

N
G
S
X
NN
NG
NS
NX
GN
GG
GS
GX
SN
SG
etc.

Now imagine a device that would read down this list of all possible strings and would pick out—select—just those that were grammatical. A grammar is a description of such a device for testing strings. If a string describes a possible trip on the "road map," it is selected as grammatical. Otherwise, it is passed over.

The fact that any interesting language will have an infinite number of grammatical sentences makes it challenging to imagine plausible psychological experiments. Can an infinitude of strings be presented to a person so that he will be able to pick and choose? We cannot write out all possible alternative strings, then require our experimental subjects to read them all and to select the grammatical ones. It takes an enormous stretch of the imagination for most people to conceive what the phrase "all possible alternative strings" might mean. The most striking characterization that I know is in "The Library of Babel," a grim bit of fiction by Jorge Luis Borges.[3] The Library of Babel, which extended infinitely in all directions and which contained everything that could be written, was occupied by a race of librarians who wandered from room to room contemplating the variations of the letters that they found. "Everything is there: the minute history of the future, the autobiographies of the archangels, the faithful catalogue of the Library, thousands and thousands of false catalogues, a demonstration of the fallacy of these catalogues, a demonstration of the fallacy of the true catalogue, the Gnostic gospel of Basilides, the commentary on this gospel, the commentary on the commentary on this gospel, the veridical account of your death, a version of each book in all languages, the interpolations of every book in all books." Joy at knowing one was in a library containing all books was short-lived, for no one knew how or where to locate any book he needed, and the certainty that everything had already been written nullified and made phantoms of the librarians themselves. Borges concluded with the speculation that the human species is on the road to extinction, while the Library of Babel "will last on forever: illuminated, solitary, infinite, perfectly immovable, filled with precious volumes, useless, incorruptible, secret."

This universe, "which others call the Library," is nothing a mere psychologist can use for experiments. Some other approach must be found. The alternative is reasonably obvious. Instead of trying to produce all the strings in advance, we must work with the *rules* for producing them. When a person learns some natural language, he does not memorize all the particular sentences that comprise it; he learns the rules for producing or interpreting such strings. In a world where no one can live long enough to say everything he knows how to say, this is a reasonable compromise.

The heart of Project Grammarama, therefore, is rule learning, a ubiquitous but poorly understood phenomenon in psychology. Part of the reason rule learning is poorly understood is that so many different factors can affect it. One might hope that experimental investigations would indicate how to organize the rule-learning process, would help us to decide which of the possible theories of rule learning are worthy of study, which are mere Idols of the Theater. Experiments with grammarama might turn up information relevant to such questions. Because the systematic study of artificial languages has proved so rewarding to logicians during the past century, it is easy to imagine it might be similarly instructive for psychologicians.

At first glance it is not obvious that there is any language whose forms you could not generate with regular grammars. Perhaps that is why regular grammars have received more attention than they really deserve. For example, at one time many engineers, statisticians, and psychologists seemed to believe that all messages in any language could be regarded as outputs from the Markov process characteristic of that language. (To oversimplify the matter for readers who know even less probability theory than I, a Markov process can be represented by one of our grammatical road maps if we simply add to it, for every city, the probability that each road will be taken out of that city—which represents the fact that some paths are much more traveled than others.) That was the model for the message source that Claude Shannon suggested in 1948.[25] Today, however, we know that although a Markovian approximation to real language may have many virtues for engineering applications, a Markov process cannot substitute for a grammar. Michael Frayn's little fantasy in *The Tin Men* could never really work. The trouble is not merely that a Markov process gives information irrelevant to grammar, or fails to give information that is grammatically essential. The deeper trouble, noted by Chomsky, is that there are many counterexamples—languages that simply cannot be generated by such systems—and among them are languages widely used and of great importance in human affairs. English, for example.

Take a counterexample that Chomsky described in 1956.[5] Imagine a language built on an alphabet of two symbols, A and B. The grammatical strings are AB, AABB, AAABBB, . . . etc., any string of n consecutive A's followed by exactly n consecutive B's. All other strings are ungrammatical. Simple though it obviously is, this language still is not a regular language of the sort involved in Markov processes. It cannot be generated by an automaton having a finite number of internal states. The reason is intuitively plain: For each different number of A's in the first half of the string, the system would have to be in a different internal state, since it would have to remember how many B's it needed in order to finish grammatically. For every different number of A's, therefore, the system must have a different internal state. But there is no limit to the number of A's we can have initially in a grammatical sentence in this language. Therefore there is no limit to the number of internal states its generator must have. Consequently a system with only a finite number of internal states cannot produce all and only the grammatical strings of this simple language.

Someone who hates to give up a good idea just because it is wrong might try to argue that nothing like this happens in real languages used by real people. But this escape is cut off when we recognize that this example reflects the structure of parentheses; take A to represent a left parenthesis and B to represent a right parenthesis. Parenthetical constructions are very common in natural languages. English allows us to embed one sentence inside of another parenthetically. So we actually do use languages incorporating this formal "self-embedding" property.

However, if we come at this problem from a different angle, it is quite easy to characterize the grammatical rules of this language. Forget regular grammars and consider the following approach, formulated in terms of "rewriting rules." For this example, we would need just two rewriting rules:

$$(1) \quad S \to ASB$$
$$(2) \quad S \to AB$$

This approach is borrowed from formal logic; the rules resemble logical rules of deduction that can be applied to construct logical derivations. In their linguistic application the rules are used to derive a terminal string from a basic axiom S; the arrow means that in the course of this derivation successive steps can be derived by replacing the symbol on the left by the symbols on the right of the arrow. For example, to derive the string AAABBB, we would begin with S and apply rule (1) twice, followed by rule (2):

S	Given
ASB	By rule (1)
AASBB	By rule (1)
AAABBB	By rule (2)

At this point none of the symbols in the string can be rewritten by any of the rules of the grammar, so we say we have a terminal string. It should be intuitively obvious that these rules will generate all and only those strings in the artificial language we described above, i.e., only the grammatical strings.

Grammars of this sort are called "context-free phrase-structure grammars," or more simply "constituent-structure grammars." In 1959 Chomsky[6] showed rigorously that they differ from regular grammars only insofar as they permit rules like (1) above, where S is self-embedded, i.e., rewritten between two non-null symbols, so that a dependency between two symbols (A and B in this case) must span some intervening string of symbols. A regular grammar admits only rules of the form $S \rightarrow AS$, where the growing point is always at the right end of the string; constituent-structure grammars permit discontinuous constituents with growing points in the middle.

The phrase-marker of a string can be inferred from its derivation. (Marking the phrase structure is essentially the procedure that the older readers will remember from their school days as "parsing.") In the example derived above, we can indicate the phrase structure by parentheses:

$$(A(A(AB)B)B)$$

or by a diagram, as in Figure 11. Examples of this kind of self-embedded phrase marker in English sentences are given on pages 87 and 113.

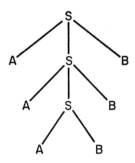

FIGURE 11. A graph representing the phrase
structure of the grammatical string AAABBB.

But enough technicalities. Merely note: Project Grammarama cannot be concerned solely with regular languages. Not,
at least, if it is to have relevance for the kind of rule learning we
know that people must actually do. Or, to put a brighter face on
it, the argument shows that there are more different games to be
played here than you might think.

How can this infinite pseudolinguistic smörgåsbord be ex-
ploited for experimental purposes? Our first idea was to expose a
person to a sample of the strings generated by an artificial language and to see what he made of them. The major puzzle was
what to tell him to do with them. What excuse should he be given
for taking such nonsense seriously?

One approach is to ask people to commit a sample of the
strings to memory. That at least ensures they will have to pay
close attention to the strings you give them. As early as 1925
E. A. Esper tried something like that,[8] and his technique was
further developed by Dael Wolfle in 1932.[36] Esper and Wolfle
were concerned with rules for forming words, and their laboratory experiments showed that people who have to memorize
words formed by simple rules have a much easier time of it than
do people who have to learn a vocabulary into which unsystem-
atic irregularities have been introduced. Faced with an artificial

language containing irregular word forms, one common mistake people made was to regularize them. Indeed, this kind of mistake was so frequent during the learning period, and again during a later recall test, that it seemed to provide a plausible explanation for analogic changes observed in the history of real languages— a psychological hypothesis for one of the kinds of change that linguists have shown to occur.

Memorization was also used by Murray Aborn and Herbert Rubenstein in their experiments with strings generated by finite state systems.[1, 22] Rubenstein and Aborn constructed strings of nonsense syllables according to several sets of rules; the rules varied from being completely permissive, where any possible string of the nonsense syllables was grammatical, to quite restrictive, where only a few strings were admissible under the rules. They asked people to study the rules until they knew them extremely well, and then to memorize a list of strings produced according to the rules they had studied. The preliminary study of the rules facilitated the subsequent task of rote memorization and, in general, the more restrictive the grammar was, the easier the strings were to memorize. Rubenstein and Aborn pointed out, in the terminology of Claude Shannon[26] and the communication engineers, that the restricted languages were more "redundant" (carried less selective information per symbol than did the permissive languages). That is to say, the restricted strings were easier to learn because relatively less information about them had to be remembered; relatively more could be reconstructed from a knowledge of the rules. However, this generalization was only approximate. Redundant strings were not quite so much easier as you would predict mathematically on the hypothesis that the amount of information memorized per unit of time spent studying was a constant, independent of the rules of the grammar.

In order to get started in this business I tried an experiment along these lines, but with a few differences. I used the grammar depicted in Figure 10, which generates strings of letters rather than strings of nonsense syllables, and I did not bother to familiarize my subjects with the rules before they began memorizing. In spite of these modifications, I was able to confirm Aborn and Rubenstein. This study was published in 1958;[14] to the best of my memory, it has been my only publication on grammarama.

It puzzled me that subjects in my experiment were somehow able to exploit rules of formation they had never studied before and presumably were unable to verbalize explicitly. At Brown University A. S. Reber[20] has shown that in this situation the learner's ability to exploit grammatical constraints develops progressively with continuing memorization of samples of grammatical strings, but that people are not able to explain coherently what it is they are learning that makes subsequent memorization easier. It might be argued that this ability to profit so quickly from redundancy is analogous to an infant's ability to learn his mother tongue, so perhaps I should not have been surprised. However, a capacity to feel surprise is one of my best weapons as a scientist and I try never to inhibit it. The result surprises me even now, even after reading W. R. Garner's[10] and A. C. Staniland's[31] accounts as to why, given the method I used, I should have expected the results I obtained. According to their analysis, the grammatical rules had the practical effect of selecting a subset of strings that were more discriminable from one another than a randomly selected set would have been, and so were easier to remember. I suppose this is as good a way to look at it as any.

After this study I stopped doing this kind of experiment. It did not seem to be taking me where I wanted to go. Most certainly, my experimental subjects regarded the rote memorization of random strings of letters as anything but fun, and that violated my personal excuse for studying artificial languages. So I gave it up. I may have been wrong. Others have continued with interesting results.

For example, L. M. Horowitz[12] added important information in 1961 when he discovered that highly restricted languages are easier only when you test memory by the method of free recall (subjects are free to recall the strings in any order they can) and are not easier when the strings have to be memorized in exactly the order given.

Another example: Sol Saporta and some of his students at the University of Washington[24] required people to memorize sample strings from two different grammars. Actually, the two grammars both generated exactly the same strings of letters, but in one case the strings were presented to the learners as if generated by a regular grammar, whereas in the other case they were presented as examples from a constituent-structure language. As a constituent-structure grammar, spaces were left, parenthesis-like, to indicate the groupings of letters into constituent strings, i.e., into the substrings that formed "phrases" in the longer sentences. People found it easier to memorize the strings when their constituent structure was marked by spaces, which tempts one to conclude that constituent-structure languages are more natural, easier to cope with, than regular languages. Since constituent-structure languages resemble English more than regular languages do, this conclusion is at least recommended by common sense. However, common sense is no infallible guide; the two classes of strings in Saporta's experiment were not *precisely* identical, so the sensible conclusion could be wrong. But I doubt it. The hierarchical structure of strings generated by constituent-structure grammars is characteristic of much other behavior that is sequentially organized; it seems plausible that it would be easier for people than would the left-to-right organization characteristic of strings generated by regular grammars.

My own interest in all this was to discover how people acquire and obey systems of rules. By and large, they do not learn syntactic rules by memorizing particular examples of grammatical strings. To put the difficulty in familiar terms: there may be some virtue to memorizing German sentences as part of your program for learning the German language, but if that is all you do, you will surely learn a very odd kind of German. If people do not ordinarily try to learn linguistic rules by memorizing particular examples that conform to them, how much of their time should psycholinguists spend studying the process?

But if not rote memorization, then what? How to make people look at these nonsense strings until they see the patterns in them? Infants seem to have a built-in interest in the patterns of spoken sounds they hear; without a comparable motive in the adult, what is a psycholinguist to do? One possibility, borrowed from W. H. Sumby and Irwin Pollack,[32] is to require people to copy strings instead of memorizing them. Copying is like rote memorization with the help of pencil and paper. At my suggestion, Jerry Hogan tried this approach and succeeded in confirming once more the general result found by Aborn and Rubenstein, namely, that the more redundant a language is, the easier it is to work with.[11] Whereas Aborn and Rubenstein counted the number of presentations required to memorize sample strings, Hogan counted the number of times people had to look at a passage in order to copy it accurately. This confirmation, using a very different experimental technique, served to strengthen the likelihood that Aborn and Rubenstein were right, but it did not tell us any more about rule learning than did the experiments with rote memorization.

Obviously, we needed a new approach. I decided to take a leaf from the book of my colleague, Jerome Bruner, who with his co-workers had for several years been investigating the strategies that people use for concept attainment; in 1956 Bruner, Goodnow, and Austin summarized this research in *A Study of Thinking*.[4] What they referred to as a "concept attainment experiment" seemed eminently suitable for experiments with artificial languages.

In a typical experiment on concept attainment a universe of objects is constructed in such a way that they can be described in terms of their values on a handful of attributes. For example, if the objects are flowers (or drawings of flowers), they might have either long stems or short, be either red or yellow, have leaves or no leaves with them, be buds or open blossoms, have one or more than one flower per stem. A person who had agreed to serve as a subject in the experiment might be told, "I have a friend who grows roses. Some of these are pictures of the kind of roses my friend grows, and others are not. Try to discover what kind of roses he grows." The kind of roses is the "concept" the person is trying to attain. Of course, roses are only one type of universe. In other experiments the universe might consist of geometric figures, and the subject is challenged to discover which ones are called, say, "dax."

When instances are shown to a subject one at a time and he is asked to say whether or not they are examples of the concept, he must use a "reception strategy." After each guess he is told the correct answer. When a subject is presented with the whole array all at once, and allowed to select which instances he would like to know about, he must use a "selection strategy." As he points to each one, the experimenter tells him whether or not it is an exemplar of the concept he is trying to learn.

Mastery of a concept can be tested variously. An explicit method asks the person to state the rule he is following, to phrase it in such a way that another person could also recognize exemplars of the concept. An implicit method tests whether he can correctly recognize instances he has never seen before; this procedure is usually called a "transfer test." A person who responds correctly to instances he has not seen during the training period cannot be operating on the basis of sheer memorization; the assumption is that he has mastered the rules or principles that define the concept.

It sometimes happens that subjects can pass a transfer test but are still not able to state their rules explicitly. For example, most of us can recognize whether or not an English sentence is acceptable, yet we would not be able to formulate explicitly the grammatical rules we follow. A similar discrepancy can often be observed in concept-attainment experiments.

Some part of formal education has as its goal to make students aware of explicit rules, and educational psychologists have worked for many years to determine how best to communicate such rules to students. The various methods of teaching rules can be divided roughly into two types, usually referred to as "deductive" and "inductive." To oversimplify the matter scandalously, in a deductive method the rule is stated before the examples are given, whereas in an inductive method the examples are given first. The question as to when one or the other of these methods is superior is far too complicated and too poorly understood for discussion here. I mention the matter only to say that all the work I will discuss in the following pages used an inductive approach. A deductive approach can also be adopted (see Aborn and Rubenstein, for example), but as yet I have not worked with it.

Without going into further details—details can be much better gathered from the book by Bruner, Goodnow, and Austin—I will assert that the concept-attainment experiment is a useful way to study how people learn the rules of artificial languages. When we adapt the method of the concept-attainment experiment to the linguistic case, the instances are strings of letters, and people are told, for example, "Here is an ancient writing system that has recently been discovered. The letters in its alphabet are. . . . Some sequences of letters are admissible in this writing system, and others are not. Try to discover what kinds of sequences are admissible."

In order to use a selection situation, we would have to display all the possible strings and let the person select the ones he wanted information about. However, the number of strings is infinite; we have already contemplated the absurdity of an infinite Library. In addition to the reception and selection situations defined by Bruner, therefore, we must distinguish a *production* situation. We allow our subject to produce any string he wants; then we look at it and tell him whether or not it is admissible. He continues to produce strings and find out about them until he has discovered all the rules of the grammar—or thinks he has.

There are technical problems with a production method, however. A serious one is that sometimes the experimenter makes a mistake. I may look at an ungrammatical string the subject has just written and tell him it is admissible, or I may look at a grammatical one and say there is something wrong with it. This kind of error may not happen very often, but inductive rule learning is surprisingly sensitive to it. Still another problem arises because an experimenter is likely inadvertently to give too much information. Even if the hints contained in my tone of voice are eliminated by using flashing lights to say "right" or "wrong," still my hesitation in evaluating some difficult instance may provide a clue for the learner. Moreover, a person who is told twenty or thirty times in a row that he is wrong has an understandable urge to strangle the experimenter. These problems can be overcome, but heroic measures are required. Before describing them, let me first review some of the work we did with reception methods.

One of the most provocative features of the book by Bruner, Goodnow, and Austin is their description of different cognitive strategies that people adopt in order to cope with concept-attainment problems. Are the same strategies used in the linguistic situation? In an undergraduate honors thesis at Harvard in 1958 David Reiss[21] tried to provide a similar characterization of strategies used to attain the concept "grammatical-in-an-artificial-language." Reiss gave his subjects a list of grammatical and a list of ungrammatical strings to study, then presented a third list of strings as a transfer test. It quickly became apparent that only the very simplest grammars could be mastered in any reasonable amount of time. Something as intricate as the grammar in Figure 10 was far too difficult for an afternoon in the laboratory.

Long ago Francis Bacon wrote, "The human understanding is of its own nature prone to suppose the existence of more order and regularity in the world than it finds." Our subjects, being in- telligent young college men and women, could, on the basis of the scantiest sort of evidence, develop remarkably complicated ideas about any problem they were asked to solve—ideas rich, novel, various, and usually wrong. Reiss questioned them about their hy- potheses and was able to formulate a rough classification for the cognitive strategies they were using. He tried to represent their cognitive models, and to represent the way their models evolved as more and more instances were received, but it was obviously an elaborate process. Reiss's subjects supposed a great deal that wasn't there, and missed much that was. Imposing order and reg- ularity on their attempts to find order and regularity was no easy task.

In 1960 a slightly different tack was taken by Eva Shipstone in her Harvard doctoral dissertation.[27] She typed strings on filing cards, one string to a card, and gave them to people to sort into piles—any number of piles, rationalized on any basis they liked. No one was ever told that his classification was either correct or incorrect. By examining what people did, aided by free use of her own intelligent intuition, she was able to characterize about twenty-five different bases on which the strings could be classi- fied. Each strategy led to its own unique classification of the strings, so by correlating the actual classification that a subject produced with each of these prototype classifications, Shipstone was able to put each subject into the nearest appropriate pigeon- hole and so infer the strategy he must have been using. She then proceeded to consider how various experimental variables—the grammar, the number of instances presented, the length of time spent studying, the number of categories used—affected his choice of strategy.

A few general conclusions emerged: Most people liked to have about five categories. The more instances they saw and the more time they spent studying the strings, the closer their classifi- cation came to the one the experimenter had in mind when she

The Psychology of Communication

designed the grammar. The amount of redundancy in the language had some over-all effect on the way people dealt with it, but the kind of redundancy was probably more important than the amount.

One example of the difficulty inherent in even simple grammars was observed in several experimental contexts. Our college students seemed unable to reinvent the concept of zero. They would explore and eventually class together a set of strings like this:

ABA
ABBA
ABBBA
ABBBBA
etc.

They might even invent a notation for such a set of strings: AB^nA, where n meant that any number of B's could occur—any positive number, that is. But not zero. The string AA ($= AB^0A$) would not be seen as belonging to this same set, "because it does not have any B's." In this linguistic context, it simply did not occur to most people to use the perfectly familiar concept of zero in order to simplify their classification scheme. However, when we told them in the initial instructions that the language they were learning was believed to have been a commercial language, used for keeping accounts among ancient traders, the association with numerical notation was strengthened and subjects found it perfectly natural to include both AA and ABA as members of the same grammatical class. In a numerical context they thought of zero, but in a linguistic context they did not.

The invention of zero was a great step forward in the history of mathematics, so it would be unreasonable to expect our subjects who worked in the linguistic context to accomplish so much in the course of an afternoon in the laboratory. But what we might have expected them to do, namely, to recognize that this familiar concept was applicable, did not occur either. The psychology of thinking is extravagantly decorated with examples of a failure to generalize, yet each new instance seems surprising to its discoverers.

Shipstone made no effort to teach subjects a "correct" classification, so no indications of the efficiency of their learning are possible. Still, people did tend to converge on the pattern that the experimenter had in mind; without explicit instruction they discovered that one basis for classification was more appropriate than others. Their first, superficial response was to classify strings by length; next they might try alphabetizing; then they might note that the final symbols also provided a basis for classification; finally, they would try to use the whole pattern, by which time they were usually close to the rules on which the language was based. Shipstone's subjects were relatively successful in discovering for themselves the pattern—a simple regular grammar—that she had hidden in the test materials.

Every subject seemed to work a little differently, and to have extensive rationalizations to give for what he was doing. It was not difficult to collect data about their cognitive strategies. Quite the contrary. The subjects poured data over her until she almost drowned in it. The trouble was that the differences seemed greater than the similarities among subjects. The particular strategies Bruner had identified did not appear distinctly in her data, and neither she nor I was clever enough to find other simple descriptive principles to account for the great variety of different things her subjects did. Instead of simple, general cognitive principles, we seemed to find heterogeneous idiosyncrasies. A sample from one subject can give the flavor of the data.

It was often difficult to decide, solely on the basis of his final classification, exactly what strategy a person had adopted or what structure he had imposed on the strings. In some cases Shipstone resorted to asking people to "think out loud" as they worked on the problem. What they said was recorded on magnetic tape and later transcribed for detailed analysis. The following sample illustrates the complexity of the concept-attainment process in this situation.

The subject sits at a table, across from the experimenter, who reads aloud the following instructions:

> During the last war an army base was receiving important code information, one message at a time. This information had to be sorted for filing as it was received. Now suppose you were the officer on duty with this important job of receiving and filing this information. You will now be presented with the same information, single message on single card, two cards at first, then one card at a time. You are to study the card and then decide how you are to file it. You can put the cards into as many piles or boxes as you wish and you are free to move around a card from one box to another any time you wish. You will not be limited in time, since the decisions you make are very important, but work rapidly.

> One further point. As you work with these cards, think aloud as if you were talking to yourself. Talk freely about what you are doing throughout your performance.

> Any questions?

"Here," says the experimenter, "are the first two cards." He is handed two 5-by-8-inch cards on which are typed

ZIR   PAG   ZIR   ZIR   PAG   NEN

and

ZIR   PAG   NEN   PAG   NEN   PAG   NEN   PAG   NEN
PAG   NEN   PAG   NEN   PAG   ZIR   NEN.

Only three nonsense syllables—NEN, PAG, and ZIR—are used on any of the cards. In the following it is convenient to abbreviate them, N, P, and Z.

The subject looks at the two cards, laughs self-consciously, and places them separately on the table in front of him. He says, "It seems as though the main difference in the way things repeat is first according to the symbols that appear and then in the order in which they appear."

There is a silent pause. The experimenter says, "You will have to tell me when you are ready for the next card."

"Next card, please."

The next card says ZPZN. He places it on the table by itself. All three cards are separately placed, so the experimenter asks, "Why did you put that card there?"

"Oh, well," he says, "there seems to be a difference in the lengths of the messages. And I don't have enough information to really decide on categories. I am just setting them aside until I get a little more information."

The experimenter, who has seen some people base their entire classification on the lengths of the messages, makes a note that length was the first basis for classification mentioned by the subject. Will he stick with length, or will he look further?

The next card is ZPZZZZZZZZZZZZZZPN. He says, "Now this card is more similar in length to one of the others I received, and it contains a large number of ZIRs like this other one, so I will put these two together, possibly in the same category." He places the new card together with ZPZZPN. Since he does not combine it with ZPNPNPNPNPNPNPZN, he seems to have rejected length as the basis for his classification. For the moment, apparently, his attention is caught by the repeating unit ZIR.

The next card is ZPNPZN. The subject reads it silently. There is a long pause. "Whatever you are thinking," says the experimenter, "please say it aloud. I know that is not easy."

"Well," says the subject, "I just noticed that all of the five cards start with the same syllable and the syllables appear to be ordered. Similarly, the second syllables in all the cards are the same. A difference arises in the third syllable, so there is a possibility of arranging these cards according to the syllables. Alphabetically, in other words. But for the time being I will put this card in with the one which has similar length, that is, with the same number of syllables, like six or so." He proceeds to file them by length, as follows: ZPNPZN and ZPZZPN are put together, ZPNPNPNPNPNPZN and ZPZZZZZZZZZZZZZZPN are put together, and ZPZN is left by itself. Although he is beginning to pay attention to the way the messages begin, and to consider the pos-

The Psychology of Communication

sibility of an alphabetical ordering, he rejects it in favor of a classification on the basis of length. He has destroyed his first tentative grouping on the basis of a repeating unit and has returned to the earlier hypothesis.

The next card is ZPPN. "Again," says the subject, "all cards start with the same two syllables. But I am going to set this card aside for a separate category for no other reason than I want to gather more cards before I make a classification." There is a pause. "Hmm . . . temporarily, I am going to rearrange the cards and put them in alphabetical order according to the syllables, starting from the beginning." The subject seems to hope that something not presently obvious will appear as he tries different spatial arrangements of the cards. As he alphabetizes them he says, "I've just noticed something that had not occurred to me before, that there are only four symbols." In fact, of course, there are only three. "Somehow," he continues, "in the beginning I assumed there were going to be more. So, now I am arranging them first of all according to syllables, that is, the syllable order and the first three syllables, and then according to the lengths of the messages." Since the first two syllables are identical on all the cards that he has seen, any attempt to alphabetize must take into consideration at least the first three syllables of the message.

Note that the subject is beginning to combine his rules in an effort to find some new basis for classification. Like most subjects, he began with relatively simple rules—counting and alphabetizing—ready-made operations learned in other contexts and transferred bodily to the present task. For some reason, however, the results do not satisfy him and he is now beginning to search for something else. As he collects more cards, he wants to come to terms with them in a way that respects their peculiarities and particularities, not by some ready-made rule that might fit almost anything.

We will leave the subject at this point, although he is only one sixth through the list of thirty cards he will inspect. (The complete protocol is reported in Shipstone's monograph.) As he worked, he came progressively closer to the classification implicit in the rules of the grammar, but at no point did the experimenter tell him his groupings were right or wrong.

Such a protocol is a rich source of data, but it is not easy to know what should be done with it. Can it be reduced to a few simple numbers, so that results from different people could be averaged, or at least compared quantitatively? Shipstone derived several measures, but they are mere shadows of the actual thought processes. Perhaps we could program a computer to simulate the successive classifications considered by the subject. If so, would that imply that we understood his cognitive processes? It is not easy to give a valid and useful characterization of a person's mental processes, a characterization that can provide a firm basis for further research.

One feature of Reiss's and Shipstone's experiments did encourage me. Their subjects seemed to enjoy it. People were challenged, they wanted to know how well they had done, they volunteered to come back again. Perhaps they enjoyed it because David Reiss and Eva Shipstone were warm, friendly people, but that was not the whole story. I felt we were finally on the right track.

Nonetheless, there was an interlude following these studies by Hogan, Reiss, Shipstone, and myself, and I did not get back to grammarama for almost four years. The very richness of the phenomena we turned up in these exploratory studies made it difficult to know what to do next. As a child I saw a dentist drop a small, shining ball of metal that shattered into hundreds of smaller, shining balls that spurted out in every direction; I had a grand time on my hands and knees helping the nurse recover as much as we could. As Chomsky and I had described it in Stanford that first summer, grammarama was a tight, shining thing, all neat symbolism and logic. Dropped into a laboratory it shattered like mercury into dozens of subproblems, any one of which could have taken years to clean up.

Consider, for example, what Reiss, now a research psychiatrist, is doing with grammarama currently. First, he has converted it into a problem to be solved by a group of people rather than by a single individual. He tells me that in his present version members of a group sit individually in booths arranged in a semicircle around the experimenter. The walls of the booths prevent people from seeing one another, but they can communicate by passing slips of paper through holes in the walls. Members of the group are told that they will be asked to solve a puzzle that involves strings of simple geometric figures. They are then given examples of admissible strings and are told that their job, going one person at a time, is to produce admissible strings of their own.

After each string is written the experimenter signals whether it is right or wrong, and every member gets to see the evaluated strings produced by every other member. As soon as any member thinks he knows the rules, he says so publicly by turning on a light over his booth. After that, the experimenter stops scoring his strings and they are shown to the others without comment. When everyone has finished, the puzzle is over. The grammatical features of the puzzle materials, of course, are of minor importance here. Artificial grammars provide Reiss with a convenient source of puzzles varying in difficulty and amusing to solve, but his real interest is in the patterns of cooperative problem solving displayed by the groups he studied.

The groups he used were families: father, mother, two children. Some families were, by psychiatric standards, normal. Others resembled the normal families in outward respects except that one of their children had a record of psychological difficulties —diagnosed either as character disorder or as schizophrenia.

The first puzzle Reiss set for them was easy to solve and all families performed relatively alike. In their second puzzle, however, the parents were given (without comment) examples that revealed some important information that was withheld from the children. How the two generations faced this discrepancy in their conception of the second puzzle provided the major focus of the study. Schizophrenic families were far less successful in achieving a synthesis of the disparate concepts of parents and children, and their performance was much more likely to deteriorate as the problem-solving effort proceeded. (Character-disorder families seemed to lie between normals and schizophrenics on almost every measure of performance.) The differences among the types of families seemed attributable primarily to differences among the children. In normal families, the parents would get the answer and stay with it until the children caught on, but in the schizophrenic families the children seemed less sensitive and less alert, until eventually the parents would give in and muddy or surrender their own conceptualization. This research is an extension of grammarama I could never have dreamed of in 1957 when Chomsky and I began.

A very different application of this kind of problem material has been explored by Patrick Suppes at Stanford University, an application not to medical but to educational psychology.[33, 34] Suppes is a logician and behavior theorist; his major concern has not been linguistic but mathematical. Instead of regarding a set of rules as a grammar, he would regard it as a mathematical system, but the spirit of his work is sufficiently similar to make it relevant here.

Suppes wants to know how you should teach mathematics to children. As part of this general interest he decided to investigate how to teach them to give mathematical proofs. The whole question of what constitutes an adequate proof has interesting psychological angles, and at times Suppes has sounded as though he expected to uncover some general and important new mathematical ideas. In 1966 he wrote that "at the present time many mathematicians concerned with the foundations of mathematics are unsatisfied with the basic concepts of logic and set theory that have been the focus of most foundational investigations since the turn of the century. A behaviorally oriented way of looking at mathe-

The Psychology of Communication

matical concepts promises a new approach to the foundations of mathematics itself." [35] This is an exciting prospect indeed, and serves to illustrate once more how heady these ideas can be. When one turns from promises to accomplishments, however, the change of scale is just as great as when we shifted from linguistic theories of transformational grammar to ZIR   PAG   ZIR   NEN.

Consider one study from the many that Suppes and his associates have conducted. The formal problem that he taught to children can be characterized by four rewriting rules:

R1.   S   → Soo
R2.   S   → S11
R3.   So → S
R4.   S1 → S

This set of rules would be recognized by mathematicians as a "Post rewriting system," [18, 19] but, even though it generates strings of symbols, it is not really a grammar. For one thing, S is a variable; it is interpreted here to mean any string of symbols, not the particular symbol S itself. For another, rules R3–4 shorten strings by deleting the final symbol; it would be impossible to recover the sequence of steps used in the derivation of a terminal string. In fact, in this mathematical system there are no terminal strings; all strings can be continued, and any string that results from the application of these four rules in any order is considered a theorem of the system.

To derive a theorem we begin with the axiom 1 and apply these four rewriting rules until we attain the desired result; since the system has only one axiom, the digit 1, and we must always start with that. Our problem is to derive some particular theorem that the experimenter selects. For example, the experimenter could ask us to derive 101 (the theorem) from 1 (the axiom). In that case, a proof, with each successive step written out in full, might proceed as follows:

11	1	Axiom
	100	By rule R1

10   By rule R3
1011   By rule R2
101   By rule 4

According to the rules we can add two zeros or two ones, or delete a zero or a one; these rules, applied in a proper order, enable us to derive any sequence of zeros and ones as a theorem in the system. In short, to use Suppes' own phrase, it is "an utterly trivial mathematical system."

In order to realize this mathematical system for a student Suppes has constructed a display of lights with buttons to turn them on and off. A child is shown a horizontal panel of illuminated red and green squares. Below this panel is a second panel with matching squares with only one square illuminated; the first square in the lower panel is always red, corresponding to the single axiom, 1. The child is shown four buttons that he can use to light up additional squares or to remove lighted squares from the lower panel, working from left to right. The changes in the lower panel that result from pressing the four buttons correspond precisely to the four rules stated above; one button adds two red squares, one adds two green, etc. Directly above the buttons is a pictorial description of the result of pushing each button. The child is told that his objective is to push the buttons until he makes the row of colored lights in the lower panel match the row of colored lights in the upper panel. It should be apparent that a sequence of responses made by the child in attempting to match the upper panel is formally isomorphic to writing a proof in the style shown above.

Suppes had planned to do the experiment with fourth-grade children (ages nine and ten), but a few preliminary tests indicated that the problem was too trivial for them; most fourth-grade children made no errors at all. So the study was conducted with first-grade children (ages six and seven), who made enough mistakes that it was possible to record something about how they learned to do the task correctly.

Their data indicated that the probability of making a correct response increased very suddenly at the time of the last error; it jumped from a chance level to perfect performance in one step, with no sign of a slow and gradual approach toward ever greater proficiency. In earlier decades of this century such an abrupt improvement was often said to reveal a mysterious psychological process called "insight"; such is the progress of psychological theory that today we call it evidence for an "all-or-none conditioning process." Without subscribing to any particular theory, perhaps we may be allowed to say that the children caught on suddenly and thereafter made no more mistakes.

It is not obvious how these fragmentary beginnings should lead on into the behavioral foundations of any mathematical systems having an interesting degree of complexity. Perhaps that is why Suppes has recently devoted his attention more to other aspects of teaching logic and mathematics to children. In any case, it is enough for me to note the range—from schizophrenic families to first-grade-mathematics teaching—spanned by the kind of materials we have been using in Project Grammarama.

The variety of problems we can probe with grammaramatic materials seems limited only by our energy and imagination. Although it would be amusing to pursue such problem variations, such sidetrips might cause me to lose sight of my basic interest, rule learning. It was certainly not obvious to me in 1959 how best to cope with the diversity and complexity of the performances we were seeing, so I turned to other things and let grammarama lie fallow for a while.

My personal interest revived in the summer of 1963 when we created a computer-based laboratory at the Harvard Center for Cognitive Studies. It had been obvious from the first that if we were to work with a production strategy, we needed a machine to conduct the experiment. If a grammar is complicated, human experimenters are simply not fast or accurate enough to run the experiment. In 1957, therefore, my colleague E. B. Newman designed and supervised the construction of a small, special-purpose computer for these experiments. Its back panel was covered with rotary switches so that the experimenter could set in the grammatical rules. On the front panel, where a learner could manipulate them, were keys that could be labeled with symbols representing the vocabulary; you produced a string of symbols by pressing keys in the appropriate order. A special punctuation key—called the "period"—pushed at the end of each string of symbols announced to the machine that the learner wanted to know whether the string he had just created was grammatical. If so, the machine hummed, a green light came on, and a counter operated; if not, a red light came on and a different counter operated. The box was so precisely designed for our experiments with artificial grammars that it deserved a name of its own, so "grammarama" was coined. David Reiss and I rushed eagerly into our first experiment with this new toy.

Alas, the machine was temperamental. It would work for hours, then suddenly fall victim to some inscrutable illness. The trouble though small was serious, for even a tiny probability of error can have a corrosive effect on concept attainment. Our technician struggled to find the trouble and correct it, but it was not easy; the machine's ills would frequently clear up just as it was being wheeled into surgery. The design was right; Newman knew what he was doing. But there is more to building a computer than just drawing a circuit diagram. Somewhere we must have been doing something wrong. After several months we gave it up and pursued the reception methods instead.

The concept-attainment approach to artificial languages, using a production method, is a good example of an experiment that should be done with a computer. When we obtained a general-purpose computer and installed it as the control element in a psychological laboratory, I remembered grammarama. On the same afternoon that our computer was delivered I programed and tested the first experimental subject. It was weeks before we were doing it on a routine basis, but at least that first afternoon convinced us that the computer worked and that grammarama experiments were possible.

Since 1963 we have automated a number of different psychological experiments. That means we have learned how to write programs that tell the machine what to do in various experimental situations. By itself, of course, a computer is nothing but hardware in a gray cabinet. It comes to life only when touched by that human spark which for some reason computer engineers call "software." Software is the program of commands that the computer executes; software determines what kind of hardware it will be. To make a computer conduct experiments, we had to develop programs and ways of writing programs appropriate for this rather special application of the machine. Some of the experiments that can be computerized were described in a chapter by Albert Bregman, Donald Norman, and myself [15] where we said that "Once a well-defined experimental procedure is developed and the experimenter is ready to collect large numbers of observations, the advantages of automation become quite obvious. Not only does a mechanical experimenter remove much of the drudgery from the process of collecting data; it is more reliable, more accurate, and often more sensitive to weak or imperceptible responses, it presents the experimental situation identically to every subject and is unlikely to be biased by fondness for particular hypotheses, and it is willing to work night and day if that is what the experiment requires." I would only add that a computer can collect much more information about what a person does and what is done to him than any human experimenter could record without mechanical aids; new insights have come from data that might not have been collected had it not been so easy to ask for them from a computer-based laboratory. Computer-based laboratories would surely sound extravagant to the pioneers who carved out psychological truth with much simpler instruments, but after seeing one operate I now know that it is the best way to do certain kinds of experiments.

Let me describe the scenario for a computerized gramma-rama experiment in order to give a general impression of how (once all the bugs in the software have been exterminated) it goes. In the summer of 1963 Michael Stein and I [17] designed our initial experiments so that, once the learner had been admitted to a small, soundproofed room containing a chair and teletypewriter, we had merely to withdraw to the adjacent room and press a switch on the control panel of the computer. From then until he finished the computer was in control. It printed his instructions on the typewriter; the subject responded by using the keyboard; the typescript gave us a record of all the messages exchanged during the experimental session.

The computer opened the dialogue by typing:

Instructions: Your task is to discover the rules for generating ad-missible strings of letters. You may use only the letters [here the computer inserted whatever alphabet the experimenter had decided upon]. Type any number of them in any order. When you complete your string of letters, type the blank key in the lower right hand corner of the keyboard and I will tell you whether you were RIGHT or WRONG (that is, whether or not it was an admissible string). If you type some key by mistake, hit the car ret key and begin again from the beginning of your string. When you have found enough correct strings to be cer-tain you have learned the rules (there are an unlimited number of cor-rect strings), type the word "FINISH" and I will give you a short test. You may begin as soon as you have read and understood these in-structions. Good luck.

The computer then returned the carriage, moved the paper up two lines, and awaited the subject's response. After he had typed some string of letters and pressed the blank key, as in-structed, the computer returned the carriage again, moved up one line, typed RIGHT or WRONG, returned the carriage again and moved up two lines, where it again awaited the subject's next re-sponse. If he hit an illegal key, it interrupted immediately to type, "You may type only the letters . . . , the blank key, car ret, or the word 'FINISH.' Try your previous string again." (The key labeled "car ret" on the keyboard was the carriage return key.)

The Psychology of Communication

What will people do in this situation? Consider a typescript produced by an actual subject. In the following case, the language he was trying to learn . . . no, it is better that you should try to solve the puzzle yourself. The alphabet contained two letters, D and R. Here is the record, just as it was produced in the laboratory:

DDDRRRDDRR
WRONG

DRDRDRDRD
WRONG

RRDRRDRRD
WRONG

RRRDDRRRDDRRRDDRRRDD
WRONG

DDDDDDDDDR
WRONG

DDRDDRDDRDDRDDRRRDRRD
WRONG

RRRRRRRRRR
WRONG

RRDDRRDDRRDD
WRONG

DRDRDRDRDRDRDRDRDRDRDRDRDRDRDRDRDRDRDRDR
WRONG

DDDRRDDDDRRRDDDDDRRRR
WRONG

RDRDRRRDRDRRRDRDRRDRDR
WRONG

DDRRDDDRDDRRDDRRDDRRDDRR
WRONG

RRDRRDRRDRRDRRD
WRONG

DR
WRONG

RD
WRONG

DRRRDRRRDRRRDRRRDRRRDRRRDRRRDRRRD
WRONG

DRRDDRRDDRRDDRRDDRRD
WRONG

DRRD
RIGHT

DRDR
WRONG

RDDR
RIGHT

RDRDR
WRONG

RDDDR
RIGHT

DRRRD
RIGHT

RDDDDR
RIGHT

DRD
RIGHT

RDR
RIGHT

RDDDDDDDDR
RIGHT

DRRRRRRRRRRRRRRRRRD
RIGHT

DRRRRRRDRRRRD
WRONG

DDDDDDDDD
WRONG

FINISH

At this point he felt he had mastered the rules. A reader with sufficient patience to study the record might ask himself whether he has, too. The grammar is simple enough. We mentioned it above, but with the vocabulary A and B. The grammatical strings are either RD^nR or DR^nD, where n indicates any number (including zero) of the intervening letter.

Before commenting on this record we should complete it. After the subject typed FINISH the computer printed the following instructions: "Here is your test. I will type a string of letters, just as you did above. If my string is correct according to the rules you have discovered, type C. If it is incorrect, type I. When you have completed the test, I will tell you your score." The dialogue then proceeded as follows, with the computer typing R and D, and the subject typing I and C:

R	I
DD	I
RRR	I
DRR	I
RDR	C
DRD	C
RDRD	I
DRRRD	C
RDDDDDD	I

This completed the test. The computer typed, "Your score on the test is 8 correct, 1 incorrect. The experiment is over. Please type your name and the date below. Thank you."

It is interesting to note that the one mistake he made was on DD, which he considered incorrect (another example of the inability to invent zero).

After the subject typed his name and the date he departed. The computer then typed a phrase to identify the experimental conditions and added a few simple tabulations. The computer could have kept very elaborate records if we had told it to, but at first we had little idea which statistics would prove useful.

This protocol suggests what went on between the learner and the machine. What it does not convey, of course, is the speed with which the computer responded, or the faith he had that it would not trick or cheat him. I find it remarkable that an intelligent college student will let a machine tell him repeatedly that he is wrong without losing either heart or face; if a human experimenter told him the same thing he would seethe with indignation. In an age when many thoughtful citizens claim to see disaster ahead for our automated society, this simple faith of the young is worth noting. The same attitude enables us to entrust our life to an airplane or a speeding automobile. Is there another way to coexist with the industrial revolution?

Now that we have seen a protocol, what can we say about it? several points come to mind.

Surely we have here discovered the most inefficient way to teach a set of rules—the way of pure induction—almost beautiful in its unadorned ugliness. Those poor subjects, working so long, thinking so hard, failing so often. Fortunately, they seemed to bear up under it, even to enjoy it, so we decided to push on. After all, some psychologists have claimed that all learning is of this inductive kind, so it is worthwhile to know more about it and the conditions that determine its efficiency.

But even beyond pragmatic questions of efficiency it is difficult to suppress a feeling that the whole interaction is grotesquely stupid. Take a college student, bright, alert, nearly educated, capable (we hope) of great accomplishments. Put him to work with that technological miracle of our age, the digital computer. What happens? One taps out R and D while the other types RIGHT and WRONG. Could such a vacuous dialogue be worth all it cost? The comment that this man-machine interaction produced a very limited, not to say moronic, conversation is true enough, but surely it puts the enterprise in the wrong perspective. Interesting psychological processes occurred during the interaction; it is these processes that we hope to understand, not their end product. The question is, what cognitive functions do the protocols reveal? It is a matter of faith that the cognitive functions we observe in this simple situation will also play a role in more interesting situations that would be difficult or impossible to capture in a laboratory. So, at least for the moment, forgive us our stupidity and inefficiency and let us look, as they say, at the record.

Notice first that the record divides into two parts, a period of general search prior to the first correct string, and after that a much more focused search for specific instances. In this sample record, general exploration occupies the first seventeen responses; in some subjects it took much longer, and with some languages it would continue until subjects gave up and stopped working. If we study the first seventeen responses, we discover that the subject assumes implicitly that admissible strings are cyclic; if x is admissible, then xx is also, and xxx, and, in general, x^n. This is what Stein and I called a "cyclic strategy." For example, consider the second through the fifth responses in this protocol:

(2)	DRDRDRDRD	$D(RD)^4$
(3)	RRDRRDRRD	$(RRD)^3$
(4)	RRRDDRRRDDDRRRDDRRRDD	$(RRRDD)^4$
(5)	DDDDDDDDDDR	$(D)^{10}R$

Even when he hit on his first correct string, he was still playing with this cyclic strategy:

| (17) | DRRDDRRDDRRDDRRDDRRD | $(DRRD)^5$ |
| (18) | DRRD | $(DRRD)^1$ |

It is tempting to think that (18) came from (17), with the exponent equal to 1.

Once a cyclic strategy is adopted you must decide which cycles you want to test. This subject, for example, tested RD, RRD, RRRDD, D, DDR, R, RRDD, DR, RDRDRR, DDRR, RRD,

DRRR, and DRRD, in that somewhat irregular order. It is difficult to see a systematic pattern in this sequence. It did not occur to him to organize his search in a systematic way. Few of our subjects had sufficient experience with this kind of combinatorial exercise to know how to do it efficiently.

Stein and I proposed the following plan to simulate this cyclic strategy:

1. Select a string x by some random process with appropriate probabilities.

2. Check the record to see if this string has previously been tested. If so, return to 1; if not, continue.

3. Select a value of n and produce x^n for test.

4. If it is inadmissible, return to 1; otherwise, exit to another program for specific exploration.

The cyclic assumption was a common one, but other assumptions were also observed. We felt that we could distinguish and define about nine different strategies: anagrams, cycles, mirroring, counting, progressing, permuting, algorithmic, random, unique. Although it is not worth defining these here, one example of a "unique" string might be amusing. A person trying to discover the rules of the language consisting of OM^nK and PJ^nL (the same grammar as above, but with a vocabulary of six symbols rather than two) tried as his twentieth string:

JJJKLLLMOOOPJKKKLMMMOPPP

When a string has as much structure and coherence as this one, it would be silly to call it random. All letters are used exactly four times; runs of length three and length one alternate regularly except to reverse in the middle of the string; letters are introduced alphabetically—all in all, a string of some artistic merit, indicating the length to which people will go when a situation is sufficiently baffling. Such responses remind us that there is more psychology here than we know what to do with.

On his eighteenth string our sample subject accidentally

stumbled on a correct string. At this point, his strategy changed. The standard response of most people, once a grammatical string had been discovered in this language, was to test next the string formed by interchanging R and D in their first correct instance. For our sample subject that next string should have been RDDR, but we see that he first tried DRDR (still infatuated with cycles?) before he tried RDDR. On response (22) he found RDDDR; this time he immediately tested DRRRD. We called this a "substitution strategy" for specific exploration; it is most tempting, of course, when the vocabulary is quite small.

We also found that many subjects reasoned that if two things worked in isolation, they ought to work in concatenation. For example, one subject discovered first that DD was admissible, obtained RR by substitution, then tested DDRR. We called this a "prefix strategy." There is also a "loop-testing strategy," nicely illustrated by the last correct response of our sample subject: having established that DRD and RDR are admissible, he tries RDDDDDDDDR, then DRRRRRRRRRRRRRRRRRRD—which is a way to test an inductive assumption by pushing it, if not to the limit, at least to improbable lengths.

On logical grounds we expected to find a deletion strategy, because it should tell you a great deal about the system of rules, but instances are few and far between—probably because the situation is such that the first correct strings are usually pretty short and did not lend themselves to much abbreviation. But even when the first correct strings were relatively long, the subjects would sometimes shorten a pattern of the form x^n down to x^1, but they would almost never delete it completely. It seemed better to talk about a "shortening strategy," ($n=1$) rather than a "deletion strategy" ($n = 0$).

In all, we tested ninety-eight people with two different types of grammars (regular and constituent structure), three sizes of vocabulary (two, three, or six symbols), and two techniques of correction (as soon as a wrong key was hit or, as described above, at the end of the string). After months of poring over the protocols we arrived at a classification of strategies and a few generalizations, e.g. (1) that use of the cyclic strategy of general exploration decreases and that haphazard strings become more frequent as the size of the vocabulary increases. (2) As the variety of symbols increases, the variety of possible strings that must be explored increases exponentially, so the general search problem becomes much more difficult. We also found (3) that the regular language we used was a bit easier than the constituent structure language we used, but nothing of any general importance can be concluded from that. And we found (4) that fifty-four of our ninety-eight subjects typed the word FINISH and took the test before they were ready to pass it.

With respect to premature finishing, some special comments are required. You might assume people simply wanted to escape and collect their pay, but I doubt it. The test was not aversive; people expressed interest in further experiments of the same sort, and asked about the experiment and their own level of performance. The true reason for premature finishing seemed to be that once they discovered a rule that fitted *some* of the grammatical instances they assumed it fitted them *all*. They would find a rule and then test strings that conformed to it; let us suppose that their rule was indeed correct (as far as it went) and that every instance they tested was grammatical. At that point they would type FINISH, take the test, and, as often as not, fail it. They would leap (implicitly, of course) from the hypothesis, "All strings that conform to rule *R* are grammatical," to the converse hypothesis, "All grammatical strings conform to rule *R*."

Their implicit logic was that if all A are B, then all B are A, which is like arguing that all men are fathers because we have observed that all fathers are men. Logicians—in a fine nineteenth-century phrase that reminds us how long it has been since they cared about such matters—call it "the fallacy of illicit conversion." It is a common mistake. Plato made it and Aristotle caught him.

The Psychology of Communication

In my opinion, its psychological basis is that same substitution strategy we observed when subjects found that DRRD was grammatical and next tested RDDR. The strategy produces a valid result when they switch variables in "No A and B" and in "Some A are B"; only with "All A are B" is a substitution strategy "illicit."

If all A are B, it may or may not be the case that all B are A. In order to decide, it is necessary to know whether there exists a B that is *not* A, e.g., a man who is *not* a father. If such cases can be found, then A and B are not identical. In the context of grammarama, therefore, what the subjects should search for is a grammatical string that does *not* conform to rule *R;* only if there are none is it permissible to conclude that the class of grammatical instances and the class of instances conforming to rule *R* are identical and that the rule is therefore valid. Obviously, subjects can never discover whether there are grammatical strings that do not conform to *R* unless they test some strings that do not conform to *R.* They must, in short, consider such predictions as, "If rule *R* is correct, then instance *X* should be *un*grammatical." But this they are reluctant to do. In our sample protocol, the last two responses may have been tests of this type; if so, the subject is unrepresentative. Most people prefer to accentuate the positive. It seems to be psychologically difficult to consider seriously or extensively any consequences that do not conform to the rules we are currently considering. Since in grammarama there is a vast and seemingly disordered wasteland of instances that do not conform to *R,* searching through them is tedious and the temptation to gamble is very strong. So it is not too surprising that many people quit before they should.

One way to describe the phenomenon of premature finishing —an incorrect way in my opinion—is to say that people misinterpreted the instructions. According to this argument, people acted as though their task was not to learn an artificial language, but rather to learn how to make the computer say RIGHT. During the initial period of general search, of course, this description is obviously correct. They are indeed trying to find a way to make the machine stop typing WRONG after every string. But, equally obviously, it is incorrect during the period of specific search. Once they have found their first grammatical string they do not quit immediately. Even though they know a string that will make the computer say RIGHT they continue to search for other strings, so this way of describing their interpretation of the task cannot be literally correct. Nevertheless, it does suggest another way to look at the task, namely, as one of learning how to make the machine do particular things. We will return to this idea below when we consider how meanings might be added to these artificial languages.

At a somewhat more theoretical level, we might ask whether the kind of learning observed here is related to or derivable from more general psychological principles. Unless one is prepared for rather unparsimonious rationalizations, the prospects are discouraging.

For example, the principle of reinforcement—so central for studies of conditioning and learning in nonverbal animals—did not seem to play any significant role. This principle is sufficiently important to merit further discussion.

By definition, a reinforcer is any stimulus that strengthens responses with which it is temporally contiguous. If we call the strings of letters that people typed their "responses," and call the RIGHT and WRONG that the computer typed the "reinforcer," then it seems clear that the effect of this "reinforcer" was not to strengthen or weaken automatically the particular response that preceded it. If we redefine "response" to mean the subvocal behavior of deriving a particular string of letters from a rule as an instance, the occurrence of RIGHT did not seem automatically to strengthen or weaken the particular subvocal response that preceded it. Often, especially in the early stages, RIGHT preceded and became the occasion for the testing of a rule; only later did the rule generate a string that could be followed by positive reinforcement. Even if we define a response as formulating a rule—as opposed to typing or deriving a string—it is difficult to believe that RIGHT and WRONG had any constant, automatic effect on the "formulating responses" that preceded them; the formulation of rules followed correct strings at least as often as they preceded them. Whatever definition of response is used, it is possible in our records to find counterexamples to reinforcement principles. Otherwise said, if reinforcement did occur, the reinforcer was far more subtle and complicated than the computer's RIGHT and WRONG. (Introspectively, it is rewarding to know what the computer's response is going to be, but whether such cognitive rewards could qualify as reinforcers is a question best left for the experts to settle. In any case, it is not obvious what behavior was strengthened.)

Subjects often tested the same string more than once. Should this fact be explained in terms of the automatic strengthening of that particular pattern of typing movements? Clearly not. On some occasions the second occurrence was only superficially a test of the same string; to the learner, it was a test of a new and different rule that just happened to have the same string among its derivatives. A subject willing to study the record could have saved himself extra typing. The typewritten record of all previous responses was readily available. Subjects seldom consulted it. It was easier to type the string again. They psychological point, however, is that they did not try to remember which strings they had tested. It was much easier for them to organize their recall in terms of the rules they had tested, for this strategy reduced the load on their memory. Once again, there is little need for reinforcement theory here. Rules were not rememberd because they had been reinforced, but because remembering them was necessary in order to organize the search more efficiently.

This cognitive explanation may seem to leave too much freedom for the individual to decide what he will and what he will not remember—too much freedom, that is, for an account that pretends to be deterministically scientific. Yet it seems to fit the facts as given by the subject's verbal report. As for determinism, if that is the measure of scientific respectability, I do not think it would be difficult to program a computer to use such a strategy as part of a simulation of the behavior of our subjects. What would be difficult, however, would be to explain their behavior without taking any account of what the subjects were thinking about or trying to do.

If the probability of occurrence of a response (string, derivation, formulation, or whatever) is taken as a measure of its strength, then response strength did not seem to change slowly as reinforcements accumulated. Rather, it jumped from unity when it was being considered to nothing when it was not. These observations are not incompatible with reinforcement theory, but the explanations begin to resemble Ptolemaic epicycles. A theorist who insists on transposing reinforcement theory from conditioning experiments to the kind of rule learning seen in grammarama will have a heavy burden to bear.

Something should be said about the triviality of the languages our subjects studied. We had to make them simple enough that people could master them in a single session. The psychological processes revealed in even this simple situation more than tested our comprehension to the limit. Eventually, of course, we wanted to raise our sights, to think about artificial languages intricate enough to be of some practical interest. It is not really necessary to teach people nonsense, even when they don't seem to mind. I considered various alternatives: computer-programing languages seemed too complicated, so I postponed that possibility for the time being; the genetic code sounded as though it might be fun, but I did not know enough about it myself to dare to teach it to others; formal logic seemed to offer the most appropriate type of artificial notation, so I decided to move next in that direction.

Logical notation ranges from very simple to overwhelmingly

complicated; the problem was to choose an appropriate level for our experimental capabilities. It seemed wise to begin with a simple version of the propositional calculus. For a while I was stumped by the stupid mechanical problem that parentheses are difficult to type because they involve a register change on the teletypewriter, and without parentheses it is difficult to indicate the intended groupings. Then one day my eye fell on WFF'N PROOF, the delightful logic game developed by Laymen E. Allen.[2] He managed to avoid parentheses by using Polish notation.

In Polish notation—so-called because it was introduced by the Polish logician Łukasiewicz[13]—parentheses are avoided by putting the binary operator to the left of the two propositions within its scope. For example, instead of writing "P and Q" we would write "and P Q." Note how this solves the grouping problem: If we have "P and Q or R," it is not immediately clear whether this is to be interpreted as "(P and Q) or R" or as "P and (Q or R)"; parentheses are indispensable. In Polish notation, however, when we write "and P or Q R" it is unambiguous that the grouping must be "and P (or Q R)"; since no uncertainty can arise, parentheses can be discarded.

This is not the time and I am not the person to explain either Polish notation or symbolic logic to the general reader. Let me say simply that admissible strings in Polish notation can be defined in three statements: (1) P, Q, R are WFF (well-formed formulas); (2) if X is a WFF, then NX is a WFF; and (3) if X and Y are WFF, then AXY is a WFF. For example, (1) if P is a proposition —"The early bird gets the worm" or "Apples are blue" or what have you—then P is a well-formed formula; (2) NP, the negation of P, is also a well-formed formula; and (3) APQ, the binary compound of two propositions—for example, "The early bird gets the worm and apples are blue"—is also a well-formed formula.

It should be emphasized that these rules have to do with form, not meaning. A WFF is to logic what a sentence is to grammar; in either case, the admissible construction may be true or false, wise or stupid. We can, in fact, state the definition of a WFF very concisely in the rewriting rules of a constituent structure grammar, as follows:

$$P1. \quad S \rightarrow P$$
$$P2. \quad S \rightarrow NS$$
$$P3. \quad S \rightarrow ASS$$

The arrow means that the symbol on the left can be replaced by the symbol on the right. Using these rules, consider the derivation of a sentence of the form P and not Q: "It is raining and grass is not blue." In Polish notation, this would be APNQ, or, since we are using only a single letter for all propositions, APNP. The derivation would proceed as follows:

S	Axiom
ASS	By rule P3
ASNS	By rule P2
APNS	By rule P1
APNP	By rule P1

At this point, none of the rules can be applied to any of the symbols in the string and the derivation ends; it is a terminal string.

In actual use, several different letters would represent propositions, and there would be several binary operators—and, or, if-then, if-and-only-if—but these are refinements that we can ignore in grammarama, at least for a start. Suppose we tell our subjects only that the language will have strings formed from three letters, and program the computer as before to tell them when they are RIGHT and WRONG. As a start, we will say nothing about what the symbols might mean, but just leave it as a syntactic puzzle. In 1965 Donald Norman and John Schneider, with my encouragement, used the computer to present this simplified Polish notation to a few subjects. No one managed to solve it in a single experimental session. Some subjects gave up and typed FINISH before they had discovered a single grammatical string. In two hours they were unable to discover by pure induction a set of rules that could easily have been explained to them in about ten minutes.

This meant that the language was sufficiently complicated. (If they had not failed, we would have introduced more symbols until they did.) The question now was this: Given a language too complicated to discover its rules in a single experimental session, is there some way to decompose it into simpler parts that can be learned separately and later combined? Most important, if we can decompose the learning process into parts, what is a rule for doing it efficiently?

At this point, alas, we were defeated by success. The computer-based laboratory became so popular that other projects displaced grammarama and so I do not have the solid evidence I would like as a basis for the following remarks. Nevertheless, they are sufficiently plausible to be worth making even without all the evidence.

The argument goes like this. If we have a set of rules that is too complicated to learn (inductively) all at once, we might be able to speed things up by teaching the rules one at a time and then combining them later. How you decompose the complicated system into simpler parts, however, will depend on how you represent the complicated system. In the case of languages, there may be no unique solution; we can never issue guarantees that this or that set of rules is *the* grammar in any psychologically meaningful sense. We can only say that it is *a* grammar and then offer further arguments to support our claim that this representation is related in some interesting way to the cognitive structure that a learner must acquire.

In order to make this argument more concrete, let me compare two characterizations of the grammar of Polish notation. One of these has already been presented: It is the set of three rules P1–3 that comprise the constituent structure grammar above. The second way to state a grammar for this language is to use a regular (or finite state) grammar. Now, for reasons I was at some pains to explain earlier, this characterization is impossible if we take it completely literally. Rule P3 is of the form $X \rightarrow aXb$, where a and b are non-null symbols, which gives rise to the kind of self-embedded construction that is impossible to realize completely with regular languages. We can, however, come as close to realizing it as we wish, as I shall now illustrate.

Regular grammars consist of rules of the form $X \rightarrow aX$ or $X \rightarrow a$, where a is a terminal symbol and X is nonterminal. The "growing tip" is always on the right end of the string, so a rule like P3 is not available. However, regular rules can give much the same language as P1–3, at least up to some finite limit. Consider the following regular grammar:

P'1.	$S \rightarrow P$
P'2.	$S \rightarrow NS$
P'3.	$S \rightarrow A2$
P'4.	$2 \rightarrow PS$
P'5.	$2 \rightarrow N2$
P'6.	$2 \rightarrow A3$
P'7.	$3 \rightarrow P2$
P'8.	$3 \rightarrow N3$
P'9.	$3 \rightarrow A4$

etc., ad infinitum.

Let us once again derive APNP, but now with this regular grammar. The derivation proceeds as follows:

S	Axiom
A2	By rule P'3
APS	By rule P'4
APNS	By rule P'2
APNP	By rule P'1

Except that the terminal symbols are introduced from left to right, this scarcely seems different from before. Why is it necessary to have an infinite list of such rules in the regular grammar?

The situation can be appreciated more directly in graphical

The Psychology of Communication

form. The rules of a regular grammar can always be represented by a finite graph with nodes for the state and arrows for the transitions between states. In Figure 12 the graph for this grammar is shown.

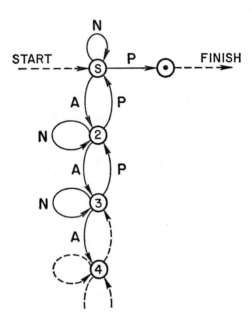

FIGURE 12. A graph of a finite portion of regular grammar for the simplified Polish notation for the propositional calculus.

The nonterminal symbols S, 2, 3, 4 are nodes in Figure 12; terminal symbols are associated with arrows between nodes; the solid arrows represent the nine rules P'1–9 stated above. Enough of the grammar has been written to allow for WFF with two consecutive A's in them. If we want to accommodate longer strings of consecutive A's, we will have to add more rules and draw more links on the graphical chain in Figure 12. Since there is no limit to the number of consecutive A's that a grammatical string can have, there is no limit to the number of rules the regular grammar would have to have if it were to generate *all* the grammatical strings. But a grammar with an infinite number of rules is ridiculous; it violates the whole point of having a grammar. We might better use an infinite list of the grammatical strings themselves.

All of which merely illustrates an argument already made. The reason for going over it again in this context is to prepare the ground for the next step.

Suppose you wanted to decompose Polish notation into parts that could be taught separately. How would you do it? Your answer might depend on which of these two grammars, constituent structure or regular, you thought gave the best representation of what the person would learn. If you like the left-to-right character of the regular grammar, you might decompose Polish notation in terms of the successive nodes in Figure 12. For example, you might begin with just N^n P, where $n = 0,1,2 \ldots$, which would establish node S. Then you would add node 2, which would be a language in which all strings of the form $(N^n AN^m P)^j N^k$ P, where $j, k, m, n = 0,1,2 \ldots$, would be grammatical—but AAPPP, presumably, would not. Then to add node 3, you would next teach a language in which all strings of the form $(N^n A(N^g AN^h P)^i N^m P)^j N^k$ P would be grammatical—but AAAPPPP would not. And so on. In this way, adding one node at a time, you might expect the learner would eventually "get the idea" and be able thereafter to add nodes ad lib, as needed.

Personally, I find the sublanguages that we would pass through on this regular way to Polish notation to be highly counterintuitive. It is difficult for me to believe that people would learn the language or think about it in these terms, or that they would "get the idea" behind the sequence, or that anything but confusion could result from this decomposition. It seems much more plausible to me that a decomposition along the lines of constituent structure grammar would be more effective. I would, for example, try first to teach rules P1 and P2, which would (again) be a language where only N^n P was grammatical. Then I would try to teach a language involving rules P1 and P3; this would be the crucial step, of course. If it failed, I might try a simpler language in which the rule S → ASP was substituted for P3. Finally, I would try to combine the two languages into one and hope that a knowledge of Polish notation would be the result.

Would it work? I do not know. Norman and Schneider collected enough data to suggest that Polish notation can be learned more easily when it is decomposed into rules P1–3; but my claim that the decomposition according to regular grammar would be little help has not been tested at the time I write this. In that wonderful cliché, further work is needed on this problem. Hard work.

When we first conceived of Project Grammarama there was, I must confess, some thought in my mind that these experiments would cast light on the way infants acquire the rules of their native languages. It did not take long to disabuse me of this idea. There are many differences; taken together they add up to the conclusion that there is almost nothing in common between the task we set our subjects and an infant's problem of learning to talk. For one thing (1) our subjects were not infants. They were young adults who (2) already knew one or more languages; a second language is never learned the same way as a first. (3) The artificial language was visual, not auditory, which accentuates a different kind of patterning. (4) Our experiments did not involve meaning and (5) there was no use for the language once it was learned. (6) Infants work steadily for two years or more at their task, whereas our subjects had only an hour or two to give us. (7) The infant's goal is, of course, much more complicated than our subjects', but then (8) he seems to have an innate predisposition for solving it that was not apparent in the work of our subjects. (9) The infant, of course, is acquiring a sensori-motor skill, whereas our adult subjects were puzzling over an abstract cognitive pattern. In retrospect, the notion that our machine might play "mother" to some twenty-year-old "infants" seems embarrassingly naïve.

A related and perhaps less naïve analogy is that the computer resembles an informant. Several linguists who visited our laboratory and played the grammarama game were reminded of the way a linguist uses native speakers when he is trying to discover the grammar of some little known language. He makes up trial utterances and submits them to his informant for approval or correction. On this analogy, grammarama might be useful as a kind of training device for linguistic neophytes. It would please me if some practical application developed. Still, I have not been willing to push for it. In general, I think the wiser course is to minimize any attempts to transfer psychological principles between the learning of natural and the learning of artificial languages.

The grammar of a natural language is a system of rules whereby the realms of sound and meaning are related. In grammarama both sound and meaning are lacking. All is syntax. In order to make the results more relevant to natural languages, we must first supply semantic and phonetic components.

At least since Ebbinghaus psychologists have argued that meaningless materials offer many advantages for experimental studies, and this flight from meaning is not peculiar to psychology. Bertrand Russell [23] once remarked that "logic and mathematics would not have prospered as they have done if logicians and mathematicians had continually remembered that symbols should mean something." Perhaps this is good advice for linguistics as well. At some point, however, it must be recognized that these advantages are won by sacrificing some very real, important, and interesting psychological problems. Future work on Project Grammarama, therefore, should introduce semantic and phonological components into the artificial languages, if only to see whether they make any difference. Preliminary attempts have convinced us that these components can make very important differences indeed.

Consider semantics first. How could meaning be introduced into a grammarama experiment? Four distinguishably different ways have occurred to me, so I assume there must be others.

A semantic component would presumably provide some kind of interpretation for grammatical strings. It would link the grammatical strings to something outside of the language itself. This link could be (1) to another language, (2) to the computer program, (3) to the computer, or (4) to things and events in the environment of the computer. Consider each in turn.

Technically, the simplest way to link grammarama to another language is to use symbols that are already well known. For example, in experiments with Polish notation, we could use AND, OR, IF, and IFF instead of A; NOT instead of N; and content words (e.g., TOM, DICK, HARRY . . . , or RED, GREEN, BLUE . . . , or SEE, HEAR, TASTE . . . etc.) for the propositions P. Or, alternatively, we could link to arithmetic symbols; we could use + instead of A, − instead of N, and integers instead of P. Since the link would be to something already known, it would not necessitate any modification of the experiment other than the use of more familiar symbols. This would be a kind of *transfer semantics;* meanings would be introduced by transfer from previously learned contexts. A reasonably definite class of psychological problems could be investigated in this manner.

A second way to introduce semantics is to assign the value "true" to some grammatical strings and "false" to others. This *truth semantics* is suggested by the logician's custom of regarding the truth value of a proposition as what the proposition refers to. If, for example, we adopted an arithmetic interpretation of Polish notation, we might then be able to write $= + 3\ 8\ 11$ as a true grammatical sentence, $= + 3\ 8\ 12$ as a false grammatical sentence, and $3 + 8 = 11$ as an ungrammatical sentence (though perhaps we might want to use other symbols in place of $+, -, =,$ and the integers if we wanted to test the truth semantics without the help of transfer semantics). It would not be difficult to inform a computer how to determine the truth value of such sentences. If the truth value could not be computed by operations already available to the computer, we might have to exercise our ingenuity a bit. But all we would have to consider would be changes in the program that the machine was given.

A third way to introduce semantics is to let the symbols refer to the order code of the computer. This would probably be the most natural approach for a computer specialist, who tends to think of the semantics of programing languages in terms of the actual operations that the symbols cause the machine to execute. In the grammarama experiment, this kind of *command semantics* could be obtained by regarding grammatical sentences as programs for the machine to execute. In order to have visible feedback that they had been executed, they should probably control some output device, such as a typewriter or cathode-ray tube. A series of grammatical sentences could then be used by the subject to draw pictures, or to copy displays generated by the computer, etc. Donald Norman has tried some preliminary studies with command semantics.

A fourth way to introduce semantics would be to equip the computer with sense organs—a microphone, television camera, etc.—so that it could react to environmental objects and events that were also audible or visible to the subject. The artificial language would then be used to discuss these things. This kind of *external semantics* is probably closer to what most people have in mind when they talk about meanings, but to do it right would press close to the limits of what commercially available technology can do at present. For the time being, external semantics should probably remain on the level of a *Gedanken* experiment.

Norman's excursion into command semantics used a picture-drawing referent for grammatical sentences. The language consisted of all the strings of the form WA^nW or SA^nS, where $n = 0,1,2, \ldots$, a type of regular language we have already considered several times. Now, however, the subject was told to discover how to instruct the typewriter to do simple operations: to type spaces, to return the carriage to the left margin, and to print the symbol #. His task was to discover how to use the letters A, S,

The Psychology of Communication

and W to compose commands that would make the typewriter do these things. By writing a sequence of grammatical strings, the typewriter could be made to draw relatively complicated patterns.

After a subject had typed what he believed to be a grammatical string, he hit the blank key. The typewriter returned to the left margin and then, if the string was grammatical, it performed the indicated operation; otherwise it typed the word WRONG. If the subject typed several grammatical strings (separated by spaces) before he hit the blank key, the typewriter would perform the successive operations in order. For example, a typical interaction between a successful subject and the computer was the following:

WW WAW WAAW SAAAS WW WAW WAAW SAAAS [blank key]

```
##  #    #
##  #    #
```

Sentences of the form WA^nW caused the typewriter to move n spaces and type #; SA^nS sentences also caused it to move n spaces and type #, but then it added the carriage return.

About two dozen people learned this simple language with picture-drawing semantics. Our original hope had been that, in spite of the fact that they had more to learn, subjects would learn faster with command semantics than without. On that score Norman's preliminary results were inconclusive; one took about as long as the other. However, a more interesting outcome was the unexpected discovery that these subjects knew when they had mastered the language. When a subject could *use* the language to draw pictures, he had a clear, operational definition of mastery. Consequently, none of the subjects run under these conditions typed FINISH and took the test before they were ready to pass it. In this respect, at least, results with purely syntactic languages were quite different from those with semantic support. Once again, alas, further work is needed.

A phonetic component to our artificial languages could also be provided with a little ingenuity and determination. Various electro-acoustic alternatives are not appropriate for discussion here, but even if natural speech was too difficult for the computer to handle, subjects might learn to vocalize in ways that were recognizably different to the machine. A typewriter keyboard is so much more convenient technologically, however, that I shall probably continue to use it for several years—perhaps until techniques for auditory pattern recognition by computers are much better developed.

If and when we have the capability to present artificial languages that have both a semantic and a phonetic component, we will be in a much better position to ask questions whose answers might be relevant for natural languages. But that would take us well beyond the problems we first envisioned for Project Grammarama, perhaps into something that should be called Project Linguarama.

Why would anyone undertake Project Linguarama?

We seem to have come full circle. Perhaps I will be forgiven if I sit this one out. It is hard enough to say clearly why anyone tried Project Grammarama.

What has Project Grammarama accomplished? Methodologically, a new kind of problem material has been introduced for the study of concept attainment, and the experimental procedures have been automated—small steps forward over difficult terrain. Substantively, the results have demonstrated the generality of certain cognitive principles that were already familiar in other contexts. It would be easy to minimize these accomplishments and to write off grammarama as nothing but an old friend speaking with a linguistic accent. Perhaps that is how it will be remembered.

Before its bones are interred, however, a few last words should be said in memoriam. For myself, the central attraction of grammarama is that it enables me to study the inductive learning of rules. Perhaps I did not always exploit this opportunity as wisely as I should have, but some features of rule learning are so obvious that even I could not overlook them entirely.

The fact that in grammarama the rules to be learned work together to define a coherent system makes it extremely difficult to

The Psychology of Communication

discuss the learning in terms of strengthening individual strings or individual rules. The importance of this systemic feature of the task was best illustrated by the problem of premature finishing. With only RIGHT and WRONG to guide him, a subject had no way to decide whether he had seen all the correct strings or formulated all the right rules. This kind of reinforcement was not sufficient to reveal the complete structure of the language. In order to communicate to a learner the true scope of the system of rules he was trying to learn, a much richer kind of information feedback was required—the feedback of pictures that the language could command the machine to draw.

When skilled behavior can be analyzed into independent responses, either overt or covert, that can be reinforced individually and assembled without significant interaction, the principles of learning derived from conditioning experiments may be applicable. Independent components, however, are not characteristic of rule-guided human behavior, and the systemic aspects cannot be avoided. Under those conditions, therefore, it seems reasonable to assume that the feedback must convey information at least as complex systemically as the rules to be learned.

Perhaps the importance of the systemic features of rule learning was obvious even without Project Grammarama. If so, it is all the more remarkable that they have been ignored by so many fine psychologists. Obvious or not, systemic aspects are crucially important, both for defining the task and for instructing the learner. If Project Grammarama can throw light into this dark and difficult corner of psychology, it will more than justify its existence.

REFERENCES

1. M. Aborn, and H. Rubenstein, "Information Theory and Immediate Recall," *Journal of Experimental Psychology*, XLIV (1952), 260–266.

2. L. E. Allen, *WFF 'N PROOF, The Game of Modern Logic* (New Haven: Privately printed, 1962).

3. J. L. Borges, "The Library of Babel," *Encounter*, No. 106, July 1962.

4. J. S. Bruner, Jacqueline Goodnow, and G. A. Austin, *A Study of Thinking* (New York: Wiley, 1956).

5. N. Chomsky, "Three Models for the Description of Language," *IRE Transactions on Information Theory*, IT–2 (1956), 113–124.

6. N. Chomsky, "On Certain Formal Properties of Grammars," *Information and Control*, II (1959), 137–167.

7. N. Chomsky and G. A. Miller, "Finite State Languages," *Information and Control*, I (1958), 91–112.

8. E. A. Esper, "A Technique for the Experimental Investigation of Associative Interference in Artificial Linguistic Material," *Language Monographs*, I (1925), 1–47.

9. M. Frayn, *The Tin Men* (Boston: Little, Brown, 1965).

10. W. R. Garner, *Uncertainty and Structure as Psychological Concepts* (New York: Wiley, 1962).

11. J. A. Hogan, "Copying Redundant Messages," *Journal of Experimental Psychology*, LXII (1961), 153–157.

12. L. M. Horowitz, "Free Recall and Ordering of Trigrams," *Journal of Experimental Psychology*, LXII (1961), 51–57.

13. J. Łukasiewicz, *Elements of Mathematical Logic*, O. Wojtasiewicz, tr. (Oxford: Pergamon, 1963).

14. G. A. Miller, "Free Recall of Redundant Strings of Letters," *Journal of Experimental Psychology*, LVI (1958), 485–491.

15. G. A. Miller, A. S. Bregman, and D. A. Norman, "The Computer as a General Purpose Device for the Control of Psychological Experiments," in R. W. Stacy and B. D. Waxman, eds. *Computers in Biomedical Research* (New York: Academic Press, 1965), Vol. I, pp. 467–490.

16. G. A. Miller and N. Chomsky, "Pattern Conception," Paper delivered at a Conference on Pattern Detection at the University of Michigan, 1957.

17. G. A. Miller and M. Stein, "Grammarama. I. Preliminary Studies and Analysis of Protocols," Science Report CS–2, Center for Cognitive Studies, Harvard University, Cambridge, Mass., 1963.

18. E. L. Post, "Finite Combinatory Processes: Formulation I," *Journal of Symbolic Logic*, I (1936), 103–105.

19. E. L. Post, "Recursively Enumerable Sets of Positive Integers

The Psychology of Communication

and Their Decision Problems," *Bulletin of the American Mathematics Society*, V (1944), 284–316.

20. A. S. Reber, "Implicit Learning of Artificial Grammars," unpublished master's thesis, Brown University, 1965.

21. D. Reiss, "Subjective Models of a Simple Finite-State Grammar: A Study of Their Attainment and Characteristics," unpublished honors thesis, Department of Psychology, Harvard University, 1958.

22. H. Rubenstein and M. Aborn, "Immediate Recall as a Function of Degree of Organization and Length of Study Period," *Journal of Experimental Psychology*, XLVIII (1954), 146–152.

23. B. Russell, *Human Knowledge: Its Scope and Limits* (London: Allen and Unwin, 1948).

24. S. Saporta, A. L. Blumenthal, P. Lackowski, and D. G. Reiff, "Grammatical Models and Language Learning," in R. J. De Pietro, ed., *Monograph Series on Language and Linguistics, Vol. 16, Report of the Fourteenth Annual Round Table Meeting on Linguistic and Language Studies* (1963), pp. 133–142.

25. C. E. Shannon, "A Mathematical Theory of Communication," *Bell System Technical Journal*, XXVII (1948), 379–423.

26. C. E. Shannon, "Prediction and Entropy of Printed English," *Bell System Technical Journal*, XXX (1951), 50–64.

27. Eva I. Shipstone, "Some Variables Affecting Pattern Conception," *Psychological Monograph*, LXXIV (1960), No. 17, 1–42.

28. R. J. Solomonoff, "The Mechanization of Linguistic Learning," In *Proceedings of the Second International Congress of Cybernetics* (Namur, Belgium, 1958), pp. 180–193.

29. R. J. Solomonoff, "A Formal Theory of Inductive Inference. Part I," *Information and Control*, VII (1964), 1–22.

30. R. J. Solomonoff, "A Formal Theory of Inductive Inference. Part II," *Information and Control*, VII (1964), 224–254.

31. A. C. Staniland, *Patterns of Redundancy, a Psychological Study* (Cambridge: Cambridge University Press, 1966).

32. W. H. Sumby and I. Pollack, "Short-time Processing of Information," *Human Factors Operations Research Laboratory Report*, No. TR–54–6 (1954).

33. P. Suppes, "Towards a Behavioral Foundation of Mathematical Proofs." Technical Report 44, Psychology Series, Institute for Mathematical Studies in the Social Sciences, Stanford University, 1962. Reprinted in K. Ajdukiewicz, ed., *The Foundation of Statements and Decisions. Proceedings of the International Colloquium on Method-*

ology of Science Held in Warsaw September 18–23, 1961 (Warsaw: Panstwowe Wydawnictwo Naukowe [Polish Scientific Publishers], 1965), pp. 327–341.

34. P. Suppes, "On the Behavioral Foundations of Mathematical Concepts," *Child Development Monograph*, XXX, Serial 99 (1965), 60–96.

35. P. Suppes, "Mathematical Concept Formation in Children," *American Psychologist*, XXI (1966), 139–150.

36. D. L. Wolfle, "The Relation between Linguistic Structure and Associative Interference in Artificial Linguistic Material," *Language Monograph*, No. 11 (1932).

Acknowledgments

Chapter 1, "Information and Memory," originally appeared in *Scientific American,* Vol. 195, No. 2, August 1956, pp. 42–46.

Chapter 2, "The Magical Number Seven, Plus or Minus Two: Some Limits on Our Capacity for Processing Information," originally appeared in *Psychological Review,* Vol. 63, No. 2, March 1956, pp. 81–96.

Chapter 3, "The Human Link in Communication Systems," originally appeared in *Proceedings of the National Electronics Conference,* Vol. XII, 1956, pp. 395–400.

Chapter 4, "Concerning Psychical Research," originally appeared in *Scientific American,* Vol. 209, November 1963, pp. 171–177.

Chapter 5, "The Psycholinguists," originally appeared in *Encounter,* Vol. 23, No. 1, July 1964, pp. 29–37.

Chapter 6, "Computers, Communication, and Cognition," originally appeared in *The Guildhall Lectures,* 1964 (Granada TV Network, Manchester, England).

Chapter 7, "Project Grammarama," was prepared with the support of the Department of Defense, Advanced Research Projects Agency, Contract #SD–187, and by the U.S. Public Health Service, Grant No. 5 RO1 MH 08083.

Index

Index

196

Index